Alexander Technique: the Ground Rules

Alexander Technique:
the Ground Rules

Marjory Barlow
in conversation with Seán Carey

by Seán Carey

First published in 2011 by HITE
HITE Limited, 10 Harley Street, London W1G 9PF

Email: info@hiteltd.co.uk
Website: www.hiteltd.co.uk

Copyright © 2011 Seán Carey

The right of Seán Carey to be identified as the author
of this work has been asserted in accordance with the
Copyright, Design and Patents Act 1988.

All rights reserved. No part of this publication may
be reproduced, stored in a retrieval system or transmitted
in any form or by any means, electronic, mechanical,
photocopying, recording or otherwise, without the prior
written permission of the publisher.

A CIP catalogue for this book is available from
the British Library.

Cover picture courtesy of the Marjory Barlow estate
Book and cover design: Vicki Towers

Printed and bound in the UK by Polestar Wheatons, Devon

hite
Healthcare Integrated
Training & Education

ISBN: 978-0-9568997-0-5

Contents

	Page
List of pictures	7
Foreword by Angela Barlow	9
Preface	11
Introduction by Anne Battye	14
Marjory Barlow in conversation with Seán Carey	
Part 1: Some History	23
Part 2: FM Alexander's First Training Course	69
Part 3: The Ground Rules	97
Afterword by Adam and Rosemary Nott	144
Acknowledgments	146
Index	148
Biographical notes	152

List of pictures

FM's hands (c1941)	29
FM Alexander aged 72 (New York 1941)	34
FM on horse at Penhill	39
FM with John Dewey (c1916)	41
FM, Lulie Westfeldt, George Trevelyan & AR at training school party (c1932)	47
FM's teaching table (2011)	50
FM's teaching chair (2011)	52
George Bernard Shaw (1928) & Aldous Huxley (1930)	54
FM reading, standing in Ashley Place	57
FM with the Earl of Lytton (1939)	61
FM and trainees from the first training course at a party at Penhill (1932)	72
Marjory Barlow demonstrating table work (Freiburg Congress 1999)	85
Marjory Barlow moving a pupil from lying to sitting (Freiburg Congress 1999)	86
Marjory Barlow (c2000)	97
Marjory Barlow teaching going up on to the toes (Regent's College 1998)	99

LIST OF PICTURES

FM walking in a field	102
FM in lunge taking Debbie Caplan into monkey (Boston 1941)	105
FM in a squat by a birdcage	109
FM working in lunge (Boston 1941)	111
FM seated with pet dog at Penhill	114
Marjory Barlow taking pupil into sitting (Regent's College 1998)	117
FM teaching a young pupil while sitting	118
FM taking pupils forward from hips	120
Marjory Barlow teaching hands over back of chair (Regent's College 1998)	122
Marjory Barlow demonstrating hands over the back of a chair (1997)	124 & 125
Marjory Barlow demonstrating wall work (Freiburg Congress 1999)	129
Marjory & Dr Wilfred Barlow (c1975)	131
Lying down with arms by the side (2011)	141

Foreword

As a trainee in Marjory Barlow's class one felt a direct link to FM Alexander. This record of her conversations with Seán Carey shares that link with a wider audience.

Observing my own children's close friends made me realise why Marjory couldn't wait to get her hands on me when I started going out with her son David around the time of her Alexander Memorial Lecture in 1965. I listened in awe to her calm, poised delivery and knew that I had to learn more. When I spoke to her later that evening to ask whether I might have some lessons, she rubbed her hands with glee and said, "When can we begin?"

After several years of lessons with both Marjory and Bill, I tentatively asked about the possibility of learning to teach.

Reading these conversations between Marjory and Seán Carey takes me back vividly to the training course when I started in the early 1970s. She was always quoting Alexander and I remember Marjory saying that everything that FM had said to her about the work was indelibly printed in her mind. In this way she seemed to bring Alexander into the room with us.

I realised how fortunate I was to be part of a Barlow/Alexander family early on in my training. Marjory had long since mastered

FOREWORD

the art of inhibition as a matter of survival – she was not blessed with an abundance of energy – and as my understanding of Alexander's work began to develop, I saw that its application in real life would serve me well at a time when I was bringing up three small children.

Marjory coped well with tricky situations. She would say that while we can do nothing about chaotic events that occur in the world around us, we can at least inhibit and order our necks to be free. No matter how strongly provoked, she never over-reacted, simply returning to a resting state.

Houseboat weekends on Mersea Island while under the scrutiny of Bill and Marjory were an introduction to practical aspects of Alexander: marching down the Seahorse's slippery gangplank with a baby on one arm and a toddler on the other; stringing baskets of beans without pulling down; learning to apply the Technique to all the little household tasks, just as Marjory had to in her early years with FM.

Family skiing holidays presented different challenges and I would try to apply the Technique while balancing on a T-bar lift with Bill (it took a brave soul) but we enjoyed the downhill slopes, singing our orders while trying to keep our necks free. I learned that the Alexander Technique was fun.

The conversations in this book are a distillation of Marjory's approach to the work but they also mirror Alexander's. She was probably his most faithful and accurate disciple.

Angela Barlow

Preface

I began training as an Alexander teacher at Alexander Teaching Associates (ATA) in London in 1983. The course had been set up by Don Burton and others, in part to bring together a generation of teachers who had been taught by those who had been taught by FM Alexander. Although most of the teachers at ATA had been trained by Walter and Dilys Carrington, there were also a small number who had qualified from the other major Alexander traditions in the UK – namely, the training courses which had been headed by Marjory Barlow and Patrick Macdonald.

When I qualified in 1986 the head of training at ATA was Adam Nott who, on several occasions, gently suggested that I might usefully have some lessons from his teacher, Marjory Barlow. He thought, rightly as it turned out, that this experience would expand my knowledge and understanding of the Alexander Technique.

It was some years later, in 1996, that I made the journey to Marjory's flat in Primrose Hill and began to have a series of monthly lessons, which lasted for some four years. By this time, Marjory was no longer running a training course, but she was still giving individual lessons and sometimes holding a class for a small

PREFACE

group of Alexander teachers on Monday, Tuesday and Wednesday mornings.

I had already completed three books of interviews on the Alexander Technique – one with John Nicholls and two with Walter Carrington – and I was extremely reluctant to embark upon another. Nevertheless, Marjory's recollections about her lessons and, later on, her training on the first teacher training course established by her uncle, FM Alexander, proved irresistible to someone with a background in academic research. I was also very aware that unless these memories and insights were recorded they would not be available for future generations of teachers and students of the Alexander Technique.

By the time I suggested a series of interviews, Marjory had already embarked upon a project with Trevor Allan Davies, which resulted in the book *An Examined Life*. However, I thought there was scope for an additional text, and so I suggested to Marjory that we should do a tightly focused project composed of three strands. Firstly, how she came to have lessons and then train as an Alexander teacher; secondly, her recollections of the first Alexander training course; and thirdly, an account of what, in one of the interviews, she called the 'ground rules' of the Alexander Technique – monkey, hands over the back of a chair, the whispered ah, lying down and so on – as taught to pupils and students by FM Alexander.

Marjory kindly agreed to my request, and we began the project in the summer of 1998. In all, we did 11 one-hour interviews. After each session, I transcribed the material and came up with additional questions if I felt that either there was some ambiguity in an answer, or there were further issues that needed to be addressed.

PREFACE

I was also mindful in putting questions to Marjory about the range and type of challenges that Alexander teachers typically encounter in their own teaching practices – for example, when to introduce a pupil to the whispered ah, what is the optimum length of time for a session of lying down, and how to respond to the oft-heard enquiry from pupils about the relevance of what had been learnt in a lesson to everyday life. Additionally, I was keen to know how Marjory recalled the way FM Alexander answered these sorts of questions, which I thought would be of considerable value to students and teachers of the Technique alike.

The handwritten transcripts of the interviews with Marjory remained in a cupboard for some years until I had a conversation in August 2010 with my friend and colleague, Kamal Thapen, about the significance of the material, which clearly deserved to be made publicly available. When I produced an outline of the text, Kamal was very enthusiastic and suggested that we work together to produce a short book. The result is what you now have in your hands.

Seán Carey
London, May 2011

Introduction

FM Alexander died in 1955. Those who carried on his work, subsequently training students, were Patrick Macdonald, Walter Carrington and Marjory Barlow. It has been said that Patrick Macdonald put the emphasis on action, lengthening and 'going up', Walter Carrington was emphatic on 'stopping' to re-educate sensory appreciation, while Marjory Barlow's teaching encouraged her students to think, to use their reason as Alexander did. Thinking, Feeling and Doing – all aspects are essential to the learning and practice of the Alexander Technique but Marjory's insistence on encouraging us to stop and think through the 'orders' before attempting any action was, for me, the way to find a systematic means whereby we could learn to apply the Technique for ourselves. Her argument was that at the moment the stimulus to act is received in the brain, the nervous system will fire off an habitual reaction – thus it is only in the moment between receiving the stimulus, before we act on it, that we can create the opportunity for change by inhibiting our reaction and re-directing our intention. FM's famous quote "Anyone can do what I did, but they would have had to have done what I did, and none of you want anything mental" tells us that his primary concern was to encourage us to

INTRODUCTION

change our thought processes as much as our physical use.

Dr Carey's account of Marjory's lessons and relationship with FM Alexander, together with her experiences of training with him, closely echo my own experience with the Barlows – I don't believe Marjory ever deviated from the 'ground rules' as she calls them. Reading these notes takes me right back to the start of my training in 1961. We were a disparate group, seven of us, though only five of us qualified at the end of three years. Apart from Dr Barlow's daughter, Penny, I was much the youngest – 22 whereas the others were all in their late thirties or older. As I remember, the training course took place in the mornings between 11am and 1pm, and those two hours consisted of intense work on ourselves. Other teachers came in to the class – Marjory's husband Dr Wilfred Barlow whenever he was free, and Joyce Wodeman (Bird) who was a good friend of Marjory's and had recently trained with her. Joyce was also a Professor at the Royal College of Music, teaching acting and directing opera students. She came into the class regularly and I found her work really illuminating. Later on Dick and Elisabeth Walker also helped in our training – they were just back from South Africa and were given space to work in the Barlows' Alexander Clinic.

I don't think I have ever been as exhausted as during this period – before or since! Marjory not only expected us to work on ourselves but taught us *how* to work – by giving ourselves a stimulus to move, inhibiting our reaction to that stimulus, sending our directions – let the neck release to allow the head to go forwards and up as the back lengthens and widens, allowing the hip joints to release, letting the knees direct forwards from the hips and away from each other. Again and again. Then to consider the

INTRODUCTION

end that we hoped to achieve. Still to inhibit any response, going back to the head/neck/back orders of release. Still to keep inhibiting any reaction – giving more consideration to the means whereby the action might eventually take place with minimum interference to the primary control. Then, if we still wanted to, we might complete the action! Or not, in which case we would start again at the beginning. All the time Marjory would regale us with stories of her own training course and wonderful anecdotes of FM and his brother AR. Marjory was always happy to answer questions – even if we were embarrassed by their apparent stupidity. As long as we were prepared to work she was willing to teach us, but if she thought we were slacking in any way she would question our commitment.

That first year we were given 'turns' and worked on ourselves, improving our own awareness and our own use. Ever practical, Marjory would ask us to consider why we should use activities such as going up on to the toes, or 'monkey' and when might they usefully be employed. Practising the 'whispered Aaaaah' proved to be immensely beneficial when I applied for a summer job teaching English to foreigners in Cambridge! When Marjory judged that we were able to maintain our directions sufficiently well she would ask one of us to come over to the table to put a hand on a fellow student's leg, paying great attention to ourselves and the means whereby we raised our arms and maintained a lengthening back. During our second year we began to learn to handle our fellow students, with particular emphasis on talking through the directions while we were working. I went skiing during this time and unfortunately returned with a broken leg which put me out of action for a couple of months. I had to work hard to prove that I wished to complete the course and not to throw away all that I had learned so far. A strong stimulus indeed, but one I needed to focus my attention!

Learning to use the hands, linking the verbal message to the experience, was something to which Marjory paid particular attention. She used to say that unless you could link the verbal directions with the appropriate physical experience you were not giving your pupils the means whereby they could work on themselves. This practice is something that some of today's students seem to find difficult – but we weren't considered ready to give a lesson until we understood clearly how to convey this understanding verbally to our pupils at the same time as we gave them the physical experience with our hands. The development of a conscious and skilful use of our own hands was an essential part of our education.

Finally, towards the end of our third year we were encouraged to give lessons in Albert Court to 'real' people. The Royal College of Music, the Royal Academy of Dramatic Art and the Central School of Speech and Drama sent students who were short of funds and sufficiently robust for us to practise on, or sometimes we were given pupils of the Barlows who had had many lessons and could be relied upon to give accurate feedback to our teachers. By the time we qualified we were all confident in giving a first lesson to someone and continuing to teach them the basics for as long as they wished to continue.

One of the most interesting opportunities we had during our training was that Dr Barlow would pop his head round the door every now and then and ask Marjory if he could "borrow a pair of hands". One of us would be designated to go next door where he

INTRODUCTION

would have a pupil on his teaching couch and we would be asked to hold and direct this pupil's head while Bill moved around the rest of the person. Terrifying, but extremely good training, for we saw how the Technique worked in practice and were given a glimpse of how to work with pupils suffering from medical conditions. This was a real apprenticeship and it echoed Marjory's experiences of watching FM teaching while she was in Ashley Place.

I am struck, reading Seán Carey's interviews with Marjory, how clearly she explains the principles and gives practical examples of FM's teaching. As we leave FM and AR further and further behind in history it is good to be reminded of how interesting and exciting this work must have been in the early days. Nothing that Marjory says here is unfamiliar to me – everything reaffirms what she taught us. In learning and understanding the basic principles of how to work on ourselves we have the means whereby we can take these 'ground rules' into our daily lives, whether that of a scientist, a philosopher, a builder or an artist. Each and every one of us has to go through the same struggle to inhibit our habitual responses to stimuli and learn to direct a new pattern of use. We cannot skip the groundwork and hope simply to learn the Technique to enable us to play, say, an instrument better – that is the 'end-gaining' approach that pervades life today. It may work initially but habit will surely take over in time. We are our own instrument; if we can apply ourselves to the awareness of muscular misuse, applying FM Alexander's Technique, we have a small chance of understanding and altering ourselves more consciously.

Dr Barlow in his book *The Alexander Principle* notes that in his early days as an Alexander student he was hoping to use the Technique to better his performance as a sportsman, but in due

INTRODUCTION

course he came to perceive that the practice of the Technique was not to 'end-gain' but to apply this painstaking method to every aspect in life. Marjory also emphasises this point: we may start lessons in the hope that our back pain may ameliorate or our juggling skills improve but the essence is not this – it is to enter into a process of inhibition and direction which may lead us into an unknown area, where we may discover what are our habits of a lifetime and make our responses a conscious choice.

Marjory Barlow makes it clear that all of the strange 'Alexander procedures' grew out of a practical need. Here is no theory – FM worked according to the rules of clinical observation and found a practical manner of ameliorating his own habitual misuse. Marjory once told me that the act of putting hands over the back rail of a chair started with FM becoming tired and stiff after working a long day and discovering a means whereby he could let his back lengthen and widen, so that he recovered his poise and energy.

Marjory's own story of how she began to work with FM when she was very young is an inspiring one. She had to discover, practise and work with the principles of the Alexander Technique, often getting it 'wrong' – and thereby learning from her mistakes – and her account of her early lessons and the first training course is a fascinating one.

In the last section, on the 'Ground Rules', she describes very precisely what went on in the early training courses, how certain actions came about, the reasons lying behind those curious procedures such as 'monkey', hands above a chair and the 'whispered Aaaaah'. They are not exercises *per se* but a blueprint, to be adapted to life situations and not swept under the carpet and

19

INTRODUCTION

forgotten because we do not understand them from today's perspective. She explains in great detail how the various 'procedures' came about. They are the means whereby we can learn to add movement to our primary directions which are basically inhibitory, and therefore rooted in stillness. In our training course she used to say that "you can give your orders until you are blue in the face, but nothing will change until you give consent to allow a movement." In fact, this is what she meant when she taught us how to work on ourselves.

There is no one 'right' way of sitting down in a chair, or going into a monkey or going up on the toes, but there are a myriad of 'wrong' ways. There are certain provisos that need to be attended to. Can you think of moving a leg without stiffening your neck, without holding your breath, without losing your head direction? Sometimes it is more helpful to turn the directions into their opposite – 'stop stiffening the neck', 'don't pull the head back and down,' 'prevent the back from shortening and narrowing.' This use of the negative often proves helpful – essentially we are becoming aware of what tensions we do not need to make before we attempt to 'do' anything. We are preventing our old patterns of misuse in order to work out a new means of using ourselves – going from the known to the unknown with only a string of mental directions as our guide. Scary stuff, as Marjory says!

We should be greatly indebted to Seán Carey for rescuing these notes and preparing them for publication to reach a wider audience. To have Marjory Barlow's memories of FM Alexander and his teaching during the 1930s is an invaluable resource now that nearly all of his original teachers are no longer here to guide us in the practice of the Alexander Technique. Bringing the knowledge of the past practice of the Technique into the present shows us how little the essence of the teaching has changed – the principles of the Technique are constant, only the application of them to life today has increased. This little book enhances our awareness of mental, sensory and active aspects of our lives so that we need not compartmentalise these elements but instead integrate them into an intelligently functioning 'Self'.

Anne Battye

Part 1:
Some History

He was essentially a very modest man. But he had a nice sense of his self-worth; he knew he had made a big discovery and found something very important. He knew it in himself, you see.

Part 1:
Some History

Marjory, do you remember your first Alexander lesson?
I don't remember the actual first lesson. You see, I had five lessons a week every week for something like a year, so it was their overall impact that impressed me rather than the very first one.

When and why did you start having lessons?
It was early May, 1932. In fact, I started not on the day but in the week of my seventeenth birthday. Quite simply, I began having lessons because I was always ill – temperatures, fevers, tiredness and so on. Really, I got any bug that was going, which was stopping me realising my ambition to be a pianist. I was what they nicely called a 'delicate child'. It meant I wasn't allowed to play games or do gym, for example. I wasn't even permitted to do homework at the normal time after school. Instead, I had to do it when the other children were playing games.

Like my mother, I also suffered from severe migraines – flashing, whirling lights and vomiting which meant that sometimes I had to stay in a darkened room for two days until the episode went away.

Anyway, there I was aged sixteen and once again ill in bed. I then ran out of reading material, and so I asked my mother if she would lend me one of FM's books which were locked in a glass-fronted bureau downstairs in the house. So she gave me *Constructive Conscious Control of the Individual* and reading it opened all sorts of windows for me. Like lots of sixteen-year-olds I was looking for something, and I suppose the philosophy in the book appealed. But the strange thing was that I never even for a moment considered that the Technique would help my back, which just ached all the time and was especially painful after playing the piano.

I had not met FM for some time so I asked my mother if I could go and see him. This was duly arranged. I then went to Ashley Place and FM was absolutely horrified at what he saw. I was very tall for my age and as thin as a rail and with an 'S'-shaped spine – in fact, FM said I had a double curvature. I was just about to start my school certificate but he said I must leave school straightaway otherwise I would break down completely.

So I went for a lesson with FM every day, and after some months when I became a bit more robust, FM asked whether I would like to help Irene Tasker with the children at the Little School. I agreed at once. I spent the early part of the day busying myself with shopping and cooking lunch. Then I would take the children to the park.

It was a wonderful apprenticeship and lasted for about ten months. Irene really taught me how to apply the Technique. It was almost like she wouldn't let me draw breath without giving my orders! Sometimes when I'd be coming up a long flight of stairs carrying a tray with food on it and she saw me pulling my head back, she'd insist I go down to the bottom and start again. I think because I was only seventeen she treated me very much like one of the other children. But I didn't mind – it was actually all very wonderful and I learned so much.

Then on my eighteenth birthday, FM came to me and said, "I want you to come on to the training course." Of course, what I didn't know, and only found out years later after I was married, was that FM told my mother that I'd never make it as a teacher because he thought I just wasn't strong enough. He didn't think I would have the stamina for all the hard work involved in teaching.

What sort of impression did the initial Alexander lessons have on you?

Well, I was absolutely fascinated with the Technique but suffered quite a lot of pain from the lessons as well. It was a different sort of pain to what I'd been used to, however. In fact, that characteristic dull backache that had plagued me just disappeared. Also, the lessons helped my migraines. The interval between attacks gradually started to increase until the migraines stopped completely within a year.

And it was fascinating to hear FM talk. I think in a way he was quite pleased that someone in the family had started to train as a teacher. My cousin Betty had tried but didn't like it and instead became a very talented hat maker. Max Alexander, AR's son, came onto the training course after me, but really he was forced into it by his father and it didn't work out either.

So when you started your lessons did you think that this was going to be a quick fix, or did you realise that you were in for the long haul?

I knew it was going to be a long term thing because I knew I was in such a bad way. I knew from reading FM's book that it was a learning process but I didn't mind that – after all, I'd already learned to play the piano and I really liked school. But I was very young and not in a great hurry, and it was a great bonus to be feeling progressively better and enjoying more energy – because of the Technique I was able to lead a more normal life rather than spend half of the time in bed. And I would get insights, of course.

I remember sitting on the tram on my way back to Streatham Hill and thinking, "Now, should my back be here or should it be there?" I was experimenting a lot in those early days although I didn't understand that that wasn't how to go about it at all. I think nearly everyone does that in the beginning. And, of course, it does take time, especially if you're very young like I was, to appreciate that it's all going to happen by thinking and not by doing. Nevertheless I got there in the end!

What did lessons with Alexander consist of?

More or less as we teach the Technique today. He worked with me in the chair, put me into monkey, and after a while showed me hands over the back of a chair, and going up on the toes. There was no lying down work from FM although I did have it from Irene Tasker when I was working in the Little School because I used to get so tired. But I found the whole process of engaging with the Technique very thrilling.

Did Alexander explain much of what was going on in the lessons?
He explained enough so that I wouldn't feel completely baffled. And I never found that he refused to answer questions. If I had a problem I would ask him a question and he would very patiently explain what he meant. Perhaps here I should point out that all of the basic things that he taught can be adapted. That's what's so brilliant about them – I'm referring to what people nowadays tend to call 'the procedures'. I've never particularly cared for that term. Really, they're all ways for someone to get good use which can then be adapted to whatever it is they want to do in life. They're the ground rules, if you like.

How would you describe the quality of FM's hands?
Oh, they were wonderful! I was so delicate and I was very loosely put together – I was far too mobile.

A bit floppy?
Total floppiness! I had very, very loose joints. I must have been difficult to work on. In fact, the only other person apart from FM and AR who was able to co-ordinate me was Patrick Macdonald. I found that the other teachers and students on the training course would all pull me around and do too much.

On the other hand, FM could get me going in a few seconds. It really was an extraordinary gift he had. His hands were quite cool and he would do the minimum required – he could get it all going through direction. Of course, sometimes he'd be quite strong but mostly it was all very subtle and very gentle. He knew just what to do to get me integrated. And he made me think too. He used to say the orders quite a lot as he was standing and working beside me – in fact, very much as I rather like to do with my students today. Overall, in teaching I try to co-ordinate what I'm saying with what I'm doing.

And the words that Alexander used?

"Neck free (or free your neck), head forward and up, back to lengthen and widen" and, very importantly, "knees to go forward and away." He said to me, "If I stand beside you and say those words, you can't go wrong. But I can't be with you all the time so you've got to learn to do that for yourself." I've never forgotten that. And he repeated that to me several times over

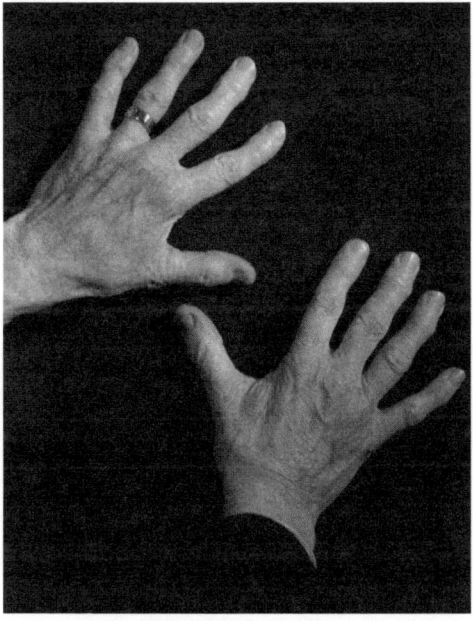

FM's hands (c1941)

the years. It shows, I think, how important he considered it was to verbalise the orders, and indeed sometimes he'd get you to say them out loud to make sure you'd got them.

Listening to your account, it's clear that you never considered yourself passive in the learning process.
You were never passive having lessons with FM. Obviously in order to change one's sensory appreciation he had to keep giving you the new experience. But very often he would get you going and say, "Now, I'd like you to move your right arm. Put your right arm up." He'd make you do something while he kept an eye on what was happening in the rest of your body. And in sitting or standing, he'd often give you a warning. He'd say, "Now I'm going to get you up. Say 'no'." But at first when it was all new I would just jump up out of the chair. At that point, I remember saying to him: "FM, I must be the most stupid pupil you've ever had." He just grinned at me and said: "No, dear. We're all the same."

Later on, when I had more experience, he wouldn't always say something. When you knew you were going to move – when you felt his hands begin to move you – you knew what you had to do and what not to do.

Do you think that Alexander had a unique insight, and that in the words of Ethel Webb, he is the only person who has truly taught the Technique?
I have heard that comment – or comments like it – so many times. But I can't agree with the sentiments that lie behind it. Really, it's a question of what FM called 'operational verification'.

For example, gradually, as I got more experience and worked on the other students on the training course it was obvious that I and others could do it – that we changed as we began to understand what was going on. This is the hardest bit of all; working with the hands is an absolute doddle once you've learned how little you need to do, although I should stress that your understanding always keeps on improving, of course. But that's not what is difficult in teaching the Technique; no, what's really demanding – sometimes exhausting – is getting people to understand what they've got to do and what they've not got to do.

You have made a good case that Alexander was able to communicate his discovery to others – put simply, it wasn't a personal attribute but a technique. Nevertheless, would you say that he was unique in the level of his teaching skill?

I think every really good teacher is unique. But I would say that FM was uniquely unique if you know what I mean. It was very clear to me that he put his whole being into teaching. And, let's face it, most of us don't have the type of being that he had.

So from your point of view how good was Alexander at getting across what was required? I ask this because it's sometimes been said that Alexander was a poor teacher in some respects because, to him, it was all very obvious and he couldn't at all grasp the difficulties that people had in learning the Technique.

I don't think that's true. If FM was a bad teacher, how come today the Technique is known all over the world? Going back to

PART 1: SOME HISTORY

an earlier point: there was, of course, another sense in which FM was unique because he'd laid down the path which then became available for anyone to follow. And we have to recognise that people vary in their ability to get other people to understand. But – and this is the crucial point – you can't get someone to understand something you don't fully understand yourself. It goes back to feeling really. Someone comes for a lesson and afterwards they feel good, they feel light and they love it. But they go away and what have they got? They've got the memory of the experience. But the memory of the experience is never the experience.

But where FM was so brilliant was in the way that he gave us the means to improve our use by thinking. The point to note here is that the bad habits we have are in the nervous system. Often people think they're in the body but that's quite wrong – habits manifest in the body, but they're in the brain and the nervous system. If that wasn't the case, FM could never have got control of the problem. Whatever the impulse as a response to the stimulus was, he realised that if he could stop it at its source – for example, by giving himself the order "No, I won't speak" – he was gradually able to assert conscious control. In the end, he only did what he intended to do rather than something being done by force of habit. He found out that he had to say 'no' to his first reaction to the idea, say, to speak, rather than saying 'no' to the speech act itself.

I think that a major difficulty is that the problem lies much further back than most people – including a lot of Alexander teachers – imagine. Everyone nowadays thinks that what they are doing is inhibiting getting in or out of chairs, but that's not what it's about at all. Instead, what has to take place is inhibiting the response to the first reaction to get out of the chair. That is the essence of the Technique.

Hearing your account I can see why Alexander said that his Technique was "simple but not easy".

It's never easy for us to sustain attention because we are so scatterbrained. I know I certainly was when I first started taking lessons. Because I was his niece, FM used to give me all sorts of little tasks to do during the day at Ashley Place, and sometimes I would forget. So after a few episodes like this, he'd tell me that when I got to the front door to stop and remember: "Don't pull the door handle. Just stand there and ask yourself, 'Have I done everything FM has asked me to do today?' Don't open the door until you're quite sure that you've done everything that I asked you to do." And in the beginning that was a very good rule for me. FM gave very good practical advice.

How would you describe Alexander's appearance?

Well, he was slim and about 5'5" in height. He was a very elegant man and took great care of his appearance. And he was very nice looking. He had these wonderful eyes – they were almost violet coloured, a very deep shade of blue – and I've never seen anyone with eyes quite like that. They were very alive and very twinkly.

He was also great fun to be with. He always had a joke or two. And he kept you happy. If you were depressed, he'd lift your mood – a bit like listening to Bach's music, in fact. There

FM Alexander aged 72 (New York 1941)

was something about his very being that did you good. What it was that he had I'm not quite sure. Maybe he was just born that way, although obviously the Technique helped to bring it out somehow.

It also helped him to control a very quick temper. My mother used to say that she and the rest of the family all thought he was going to murder someone one day. She used to tell us that if as a young man he ever saw anybody being cruel to an animal or another human being he would go mad and become totally uncontrolled. But it was that quality – that energy – that he was able to harness into this very wonderful way of being.

If you walked down the street behind him – and this was true right to the end of his life – he had the figure and walk of a young man.

Where do you think that energy came from?
It's very difficult to say how much could be put down to endowment, upbringing and how much to the Technique. Although he was always ill as a child, he was nevertheless brought up in the backwoods of Tasmania and he enjoyed a very natural outdoor life as a child. Tasmania has a wonderful climate so it's a very good place to grow up. And his mother had very firm ideas about good food. Although they weren't very well off they did live on a farm, which meant they were able to access some very nutritious fare. So on separate days of the week, the family had liver, kidneys, tripe and so on. Indeed, throughout his life FM was very particular about his food – he didn't eat an awful lot but he insisted that what he did eat had to be top quality.

As I said, we know that as a child and as a young man he suffered from ill health. But later on in life it was quite different and he enjoyed very good health. He'd pick up the odd cold or two but he always got over them very quickly. However, he always looked pale – he wasn't one of those ruddy faced creatures. And he used himself so well too – he was very economical with his energy and had great stamina. He used to say to us, "Sometimes you have to try not to take more than ten pupils a day."

Of course, he himself would often do much more than this. He used to start at nine o'clock having had a cup of cocoa which I used to make for him, work until one, take lunch until two, then work from two until four, take tea and start again at four-thirty and work until six-thirty or so. A lesson was half an hour so FM was giving 15 or 16 lessons a day every weekday. And he also worked on Saturday morning. When the training course was on, two hours of his normal day would be devoted to teaching us. It was a very demanding routine that he gave himself. But nevertheless he had this sparkle, and displayed an immense enjoyment of life.

He obviously liked teaching, then.
Absolutely. He was completely fascinated by it. He never got bored. It's the same with me. I've been studying the Technique for 65 years and I'm just as intrigued by it all now as when I first started. Of course, it's such fun when you become really skilful. And I've always loved using my hands – it's why I love playing the piano.

From your point of view, how would you assess Alexander's personality: was he gregarious or a bit of a loner?
I think he was a bit of both. As a young man he'd been a bit of a loner, not least because he was always getting ill. But if he hadn't suffered in that way and also been fairly self-sufficient, he'd never have undergone that discipline in discovering the Technique. His family thought he was crazy spending hour after hour gazing at himself in those mirrors. In fact, the only person who really believed in him was his mother, although she never understood to the day she died what he'd been up to. Her

attitude was: "Whatever Freddy does is all right." He was her first, you see – the first of eight children.

In her eyes, he was the top man.
Absolutely.

From a slightly different angle: would you say FM was an introvert or an extrovert?
He was very difficult to categorise, really. He was very balanced. For instance, he would take part acting in a play and enjoy every minute of it. But then he'd be quite content to be by himself as well. I remember when he was in his 80s he said to me, "You know dear, I'm always happy." I didn't understand what he meant at the time but I do now. In many ways, he had a terrible life, but he had something steady inside. I don't know what you would call it, but whatever it was, it was never pushed or shaken.

In fact, he wrote something about this in *Man's Supreme Inheritance* – about why happiness was so rare amongst adults in the modern world. From his point of view, people put an awful lot of energy into misusing themselves. He saw this tendency as one of the major barriers to happiness. I think a lot of people in our society experience a profound lack of meaning – they just live from day to day: they're not going anywhere and they don't wonder why they're here. In fact, many of them experience a terrible emptiness, and so they want excitement of one form or another, whether it's from drink, drugs or something else.

But according to FM, happiness is to be found in the

ordinary, little things in life. And in his case he had a great capacity to enjoy things like food about which, as I've said already, he was very discriminating. In fact, after I had been at Ashley Place for some time I used to cook his lunch. This meant going up to the Army & Navy Stores on Victoria Street to get the food and then preparing and cooking it. FM liked simple cuisine – something like a grilled piece of salmon was all he wanted. And it was the same with wine. He knew quite a lot about wine and he'd normally have a glass with his evening meal. But he was moderate in everything. He was a natural Zen-type person. And I learned such a lot from him – not just about the Technique but also about living.

He also had a keen interest in horses, didn't he?

Yes, because he'd been born and brought up with them on the farm belonging to his grandfather. Horses were his daily companions. He loved them. And he had a wonderful eye for a horse. I've always maintained that his interest in racing was his light relief because most of his life was so serious – he was dealing with people with such tremendous problems – and horses were a sort of balance for his sanity. And there is no doubt that he enjoyed having that little bit of excitement on racing days. He got tremendous pleasure from it. Almost every Saturday he would go to the races.

Did you ever accompany him?

Sometimes he'd send a car for us on big days like the running of the Derby at Epsom. But I didn't go regularly because I lived in Sidcup and my weekends were spent there. There's no doubt

FM on horse at Penhill

that he loved pitting his wits against the bookies. I think his attitude was, 'Some you win, some you lose.' I think over the course of the year he'd end up pretty much evens.

What was Alexander's attitude to religion?

Well, I would say he was basically the most religious man I've ever met although not in the sense of holding on to a particular dogma or belonging to a church. Of course, when he was a boy he went to church – in fact, the family practically lived in church on a Sunday. Perhaps I should point out that it was all fairly Low Church, non-conformist stuff – that was the family background, after all. And he carried on attending services until one of his younger brothers developed meningitis and screamed and screamed in agony. FM prayed for him but the poor boy died. And that made him think. So FM was very keen on people taking responsibility for their actions and activities – he didn't expect God to do everything.

But having said that, there is no doubt that he had a great sense of purpose.

So, looking back do you think that Alexander felt there was meaning to the universe, or was he of the opinion that human beings spin webs of significance in order to create meaning – in other words that the universe is a blank canvas on which we paint our pictures?

It's not a question I can answer directly, but my impression was that he thought we inhabited an intelligent universe. I don't think he would have been any more specific than that. Indeed, he would never answer questions about religion. He used to say, "I believe everything and I believe nothing." Of course, people were always trying to pin him down. They would say, "FM, do you believe in God?" Or, "Are you a Christian?" You see people always want to shift the responsibility to someone else so that they could say, "FM says…" and then some people would believe it because he had said it.

That's interesting. Do you think he ever saw himself as an authority figure?

No, not at all. He was essentially a very modest man. But he had a nice sense of his self-worth; he knew he had made a big discovery and found something very important. He knew it in himself, you see. He'd gone from being this rather useless, feeble creature into being quite a chap. He used to tell us that in his own field – the use of the human organism – he knew what was what. But he didn't pretend to be an expert in any other field, though he would criticise people if they weren't adhering to the principles he believed in or knew were true. Take physical culture, for example. If people were making false or misleading claims he would point this out. He spoke of what he knew, and you can't ask for fairer than that.

Now, he gave lessons to some very eminent people – George Bernard Shaw, Aldous Huxley, and John Dewey, for example – so do you think these encounters were important for his self-image, and his sense of self-worth?

He was always very pleased when anyone well-known came to him because he saw it as being important for the work. But he

FM with John Dewey (c1916)

PART 1: SOME HISTORY

didn't take it personally. It was never 'my work' but 'the work'. Having said that, I think a lot of people became enthusiastic about the Technique because of FM's personality.

Why do you think that was?
I think one very important factor is that people trusted him – they felt safe. I mean it was the Edwardian era and he would make the women who came along for lessons go into the bathroom at Ashley Place and take off their corsets because he couldn't work on them if they had them in place. It's really extraordinary when you think about it because in those days men didn't touch women unless they were their husbands. For the most part, society was very strict and very formal. But there is no doubt that people trusted FM once they had contact with him. And he was perfectly professional and never stepped over the mark – he had very strict and definite ideas about what was ethical and correct behaviour. And remember most of the people who came to him had quite serious things wrong with them – often they had been everywhere else and spent a small fortune in doing so, yet had not derived any benefits.

But isn't it also the case that he didn't suffer fools gladly?
That's right. But if you were like me – pretty slow and stupid on the uptake but nevertheless trying your very best – he would be incredibly patient. He never once got angry with me, and I was with him more or less every day for eight years. However, if he thought you were messing about and not doing what you should be doing then you'd get a rocket. And he could get very angry. We used to say that he consciously controlled himself

into a rage. You see he was an actor, a born actor. Sometimes he would get me to check his pulse when he was doing one of his rages. And what was remarkable was that his pulse was as regular as it was under normal circumstances. As I said earlier, there was something inside him that wasn't disturbed by whatever was going on. So he could get angry if the provocation was there, but it didn't upset him physically.

You clearly found him very approachable.
Oh yes! A lot of people were terribly in awe of him. I remember Erika Whittaker once telling me that she preferred having work with AR because she wasn't in awe of him. But I didn't feel anything like that with FM. For example, if I had a question I'd just ask him. And he never refused to answer one about the Technique because he knew that I was asking because I wanted to know something. And I think he was very pleased that a member of the family should be so interested in the work.

Does this mean that as his niece you had privileged access to him?
I was very careful about that. I looked upon him as my teacher and I was his student just like anybody else. And I never traded on that. I never wanted any reflected glory.

So you only asked him questions in a lesson or on the training course?
Oh no! You see, I was with him a lot outside the training course. We used to go on holiday together. I'd take him up to North Wales. We used to ride horses all over those lovely hills. On

43

those occasions, I used to talk to him endlessly about the work. Looking back, he must have got sick of my questions but if he was he never showed it.

And he'd often invite me over to dinner. This was absolutely lovely because he wouldn't let me lift a finger. He would sit me down at the kitchen table at Ashley Place and talk to me while he cooked the entire meal. Then he'd say, "Come on dear!" and then take his keys and we would go down to the cellar and he'd ask what sort of wine I'd like to drink. This sort of event would happen after I'd been working very hard, for example, and it was a kind of reward.

I look back on these occasions as very special times. In a way, he didn't treat me like a niece but as someone who was very keen about his work. So our relationship was different from the conventional uncle-niece relationship. It had that extra dimension. He wasn't like my other uncles. He was special. And as I said earlier I saw him as my teacher.

But, as you've indicated, there was some family sentiment too.

Of course. I was very fond of him. Sometimes if we were having tea or something I'd say, "Oh, I do love you FM" and give him a big hug. And he was a very affectionate man. He never forgot a birthday, and at the end of the year he would write a little note to each of us telling us how thankful he was for our help and support throughout the year. And he was a great letter writer too. If he received a letter, he would reply almost immediately.

He was also a very generous man. Anybody in the family

who was in any sort of difficulty or trouble would go to FM and he would help them out. And he had all these unmarried sisters – Aunty Mary and Aunty May – who didn't have any way of earning a living. So he supported them. He had a terrific feeling for the family.

My father died in 1932 with cancer and there wasn't any money because my mother, FM's sister, had let my father's life assurance lapse. So FM bought a lot of our furniture for us, gave my mother an allowance and provided me with a season ticket so I could travel up from Sidcup to London each day. He just took care of us.

Did he ever talk about his life in Australia? Did he ever indicate to you that he missed his homeland?

I think he did miss it, and I think I can understand why, having been to Tasmania and been to where he was born. It really is the most beautiful country I've ever visited. All the little roads around the farm where they lived at Table Cape are where he used to go riding. And he used to talk a lot about his father who undoubtedly was a brilliant horseman. He also had tremendous admiration for him, and he obviously adored his mother.

But he never returned to the place of his birth.

That's quite right. Nowadays international travel is so much easier but in those days it was a very complicated affair. And you see he had a lot of responsibilities to his family and other people in this country. So I think he thought that Tasmania was an important part of his life, but he was content living in England.

PART 1: SOME HISTORY

Now Alexander had set out with a burning ambition to become an actor. Then after discovering the Technique he changed direction and became a teacher working alone with a pupil for the most part. Do you think he missed the applause and the adulation that success in the theatre provides?

By the time he'd come to England he realised that he was in possession of a great treasure. No one else but he could do it, after all. But actors are two a penny, aren't they? However, if it had not been for that tremendous emotional drive to be a great actor, he could never have done what he did. That's what's so interesting. You have to have that emotional thing – that emotional drive – in order to discover that new pathway and keep you going, especially in the hard times.

Earlier you mentioned FM's brother, Albert Redden Alexander, more familiarly known as AR. What was he like?

AR was a very interesting man and a much bigger, bulkier and stockier man than FM who was very fine-boned. But it was FM's proud boast that he had never put his hands on him. AR had taught himself by watching FM, reading FM's books, and talking with FM, and finally working on himself. The two brothers were very close but totally different characters. AR had had a very adventurous life – he'd been gold prospecting and enlisted in the British Army where he accidentally shot off one of his fingers. But like FM, AR had a great appetite for living. Then, of course, he was thrown from his horse riding in Hyde Park and was told he would never walk again – although

I always say you should never say something like that to an Alexander person because AR proved the doctors wrong and did walk again, although he always had a slight limp and used a walking stick.

I'm puzzled why FM never put his hands on AR; surely that would have been a huge advantage to AR in learning the Technique. How do you see it?

Have I ever told you how FM came to use his hands in teaching? No? Well, after FM recovered his voice, he earned part of his living teaching drama students. I remember him telling me: "It never occurred to me that they wouldn't be able to do what I told them. But they just couldn't understand what I was talking about. So when they pulled their heads back, I just put my hands on and made an adjustment." Later on, of course, he

FM, Lulie Westfeldt, George Trevelyan & AR at training school party (c1932)

realised that it was because their sensory appreciation was so awful that he was having trouble getting the explanation across. But the way he used his hands was kind of instinctive at first.

Now with AR, I think it must have had a lot to do with their sibling relationship. AR obviously thought, "Well, to hell with this! If he can do it, I can do it too!" And we have to remember that FM wouldn't put his hands on someone unless he'd been invited to – he didn't push the Technique at you at all. And I think FM admired AR for his attitude that he would work it out for himself. He loved people to be their own sort of person. In fact, with me he never offered any advice about what I should do. He used to say, "You've got to find your own way. Each person has to find their own path in life." And he was true to his word. For instance, he stood by and watched me make some awful mistakes in my life, which was really remarkable now that I think about it. You see, after my father had died FM was almost *in loco parentis*. Yet he never asserted his authority. In fact, he was always a very courteous man. He'd been brought up very well.

But back to AR. I must say that he had wonderful hands. They were quite different to FM's. They were quite gentle and gave you wonderful direction. AR was very keen on getting the pupil to think. And he could tell in a second if you weren't directing. In fact, AR could be quite tough. A lot of people were fairly frightened of him because of this.

So how did AR's teaching style differ from FM's ?

He was very insistent you work on yourself. For example, both

FM and AR would take you back in sitting from upright so that you were leaning against the back of the chair at an angle. But FM would always help you to come back to upright whereas AR would stand out in front and say, "Now, come forward." But that's a very difficult thing to do on your own. And AR would very definitely point it out if someone wasn't thinking while carrying out the process.

Incidentally, is this why you have developed the method of getting the pupil to put the knees away in returning to upright from the back of the chair?
Well, you are meant to be giving the orders for the knees to go forward from the hips and away from each other. But I've found that if you actually get people to move the knees forward and away a little bit it does help. It sort of distracts someone from the horror of the situation!

I understand that AR was very insistent that his pupils should read FM's books.
Yes. He would always recommend that pupils read the books. And sometimes he insisted on it.
For example, he would get his son, Max, my sister and me to sit on the lawn with a copy of *Man's Supreme Inheritance* and read aloud passages from it to each other. The others didn't like doing it, but I did.

Did AR use the same teaching methods as FM?
Yes. Monkey, hands over the back of a chair, whispered ahs, going up on the toes and so on.

And table work?

Well, there was only one table at Ashley Place. It was in the back room which we used to call the 'Black Hole of Calcutta' because it was so dark. The students mainly worked on each other on the floor. And AR would help us with that. And, of course, he'd use the chair. He'd sit beside you on a rather nice upholstered Victorian stool. He'd take you back and forward on the chair quite a lot.

I think that the main thing I learned from AR was how important the messages going from the brain and nervous system were. He emphasised it in a way that made me sit up and take notice. FM emphasised it too but I think I understood it better from AR because he insisted on you thinking in a way that FM didn't insist. Looking back, I count myself extremely lucky that after my initial lessons with FM, I alternated between the two of them, which gave me a very rounded

FM's teaching table (2011)

re-educational experience. This meant that by the time I entered the training course I knew how to apply the Technique to everyday things. It was a great advantage.

Alexander worked at Ashley Place in Victoria for most of his life. The building suffered extensive damage in the Second World War, and it has long since been demolished. But what sort of place was it?

It was a small suite of rooms in a mansion block almost opposite Westminster Cathedral. There was a flight of stairs leading up to the front door. And there was a very clever arrangement that everyone had to learn to get into the building. You had to push open a little side window, put your hand through and then open the front door from the inside. Anyone FM trusted knew about this procedure – it avoided ringing the bell and getting someone to come and open the door.

Inside, it was very dark and old-fashioned. The apartment was divided into a ground floor and a basement with steps leading into a small courtyard. The ground floor consisted of FM's teaching room adjacent to which was his secretary Ethel Webb's room. The door between the two rooms was always kept open. Then there was a bathroom and a waiting room opposite the front door. If you went along the corridor, this led you to the Black Hole of Calcutta. There was also a big teaching room with a coal fireplace and next to it another room which had sliding doors. The students on the training course used the first of these big rooms, while the Little School occupied the other. When we weren't having a class, AR used the training course room as his teaching room.

PART 1: SOME HISTORY

FM's teaching chair (2011)

Next to the Black Hole of Calcutta was a flight of stairs leading to the basement. This area contained FM's bedroom, a big bathroom, the dining room and the kitchen. Sometimes if we were pushed for space we had to use the dining room to teach in as well. Overall, there wasn't a lot of room at Ashley Place. And it was because of this that I learned to give a lesson for half an hour on the dot. If you went on too long the whole day's schedule would have been thrown out of gear for everyone.

It was also a very lively sort of place. There was always lots of laughter and lots of fun. And FM used to make a lot of noise if he had someone like George Bernard Shaw in for a lesson. You'd hear roars of laughter coming from the room. We used to send someone along to say, "Would Mr. Alexander please not make so much noise because he's disturbing the students"! Then a bit later on FM would send some sort of message back to us, which would make us laugh. As I said, it was great fun.

So you encountered George Bernard Shaw, then.
Yes. George Bernard Shaw was very friendly. He liked to come in for his lesson a bit early so that he could talk to the students. He was really interested in the work and so he was very keen to find out how we were getting along.

Did you meet Aldous Huxley as well?
I remember the first day that Aldous Huxley came for a lesson very well. I had just come back from the bank, and he was sitting in the waiting room. He was an immensely tall man and he was wearing a sort of sombrero hat. He was sagging although he wasn't doing that the next time I saw him, I promise you! But that first encounter with him – he really was the most appalling sight. This very tall man totally screwed down into himself.

In fact, Aldous had a son called Matthew who was then about 14 or 15 years of age. When it was time for his next birthday party, Aldous got me to go and help his wife and hand out cakes and cups of tea to the guests. Then he put in an appearance at the end as he didn't want to be the centre of attention. I got to know the family quite well – they had a house in Piccadilly.

How many lessons did Huxley and Shaw have?

They both came regularly over a long period. In fact, Shaw continued having lessons for the rest of his life. When Huxley moved to America he continued to have lessons from other teachers.

So neither of them just came for a course of thirty or so lessons?

There was no such thing as thirty lessons in those days. If people asked, "How many lessons am I going to need?" FM would reply: "We'll have to work and see. To a certain extent it is up to you how deeply you want to go into it." FM would never prejudge a situation. Moreover, it would have been impossible for him to know in advance how quickly anyone was going to learn – how kinaesthetically intelligent they were, in other

George Bernard Shaw (1928) & Aldous Huxley (1930)

words – or where they wanted to go with the Technique.

But FM was always very insistent that when people first came for lessons, they came every day. In fact, he wouldn't take them on unless they came five days – and sometimes six days – a week. And FM didn't allow us to take people unless they came every day either. With FM, pupils came every day for four weeks and then the frequency would be reduced gradually.

Do you know what Alexander thought of Huxley's and Shaw's progress with the Technique?

He was very pleased with the progress of both of them. As you know, Shaw was a very committed vegetarian but FM didn't like the feel of him – he thought there was something wrong – and FM's diagnosis was that he was anaemic. He thought that Shaw needed something like a good meal of liver, which would provide plenty of protein and iron. So he suggested this to Mrs Shaw, who was also coming for lessons. But she said, "Don't say anything like that to GB because you'll never see him again if you do. He'll just take off!"

FM wasn't satisfied with that response so he very gently broached the subject with Shaw, and to his surprise found that he was very amenable to the suggestion and that he said he would consider it. Soon afterwards, Shaw was carted off to hospital and actually given liver injections because he was so ill on account of his anaemia. Looking back, I think it was very clever of FM to have given an accurate diagnosis. And suggesting that Shaw might need some liver made no difference to their friendship. I think Shaw appreciated FM's concern. It's no fun being anaemic. I've been there, I know!

Alexander disagreed with some of Huxley's enthusiasms like the Bates Method. Do you know the reasons?

Well, he didn't like the Bates Method because he considered that there were certain things about it that were anti-Alexander – that it made it very difficult for people to keep the work going, which was what FM was primarily interested in. I don't think he held it against Huxley; rather, he just said to him what he thought about Bates. It was up to Huxley then to make up his own mind about its merits.

Did Alexander become aware of Huxley's experiments with mescaline and LSD after his move to America?

I can't remember. But FM wouldn't have approved. Nevertheless, he had a great affection and admiration for Huxley. He was, after all, a man of great intellect and FM found it very stimulating to work with him.

Nowadays, the Technique is often synonymous with the alleviation of back pain. But when you were at Ashley Place what sort of problems was Alexander being asked to help with?

He had to deal with everything. And the wonderful thing about FM was that he never said to himself, "I've never dealt with this particular condition before, it may not work." Instead, he said: "I've not dealt with this before. Let's see what the work can do." And he would explain to the pupil that he'd never taken anyone with that condition before but that learning the Technique would certainly help with life in general, and it might well alleviate the condition they were suffering with. So he always

FM reading, standing in Ashley Place

gave the work a chance. I think if he hadn't done that, we young teachers would never have dared to take asthmatics and so on for lessons. But we knew from FM's example that if we got the co-operation of the pupil anything was possible.

I remember the first time I took someone – she was a singer with a terrible scoliosis – who wanted to go and study music at college and had ambitions to become an opera singer. But she couldn't stand without hanging on to the piano. I had a long talk with her and said: "Look, I've never had a case like this before. Are you prepared to come every day until we get to the point where you can work on yourself?" To which she replied, "I'll do anything." And do you know that she took the audition the following term and got her place in college! All she needed was a back that worked and provided support so that she could give a good vocal performance.

These days a lot of people coming for an introductory course of lessons are only given one lesson a week. What's your view?

I think it's completely the wrong way to go about things. But then I'm old-fashioned. However, I'm not alone in this. Indeed, FM used to say that it was very important to give pupils a very concentrated teaching experience because they were up against their habits, which if they were having one lesson a day meant that they were practising their habitual way of going about things twenty-three and a half hours out of twenty-four. And I must emphasise that teaching in that concentrated way allowed FM to get extraordinary results. I think that the absolute minimum a new pupil should start with is three lessons a week.

The other requirement FM made of pupils was that they should read one of his books. At his initial interview with a pupil he'd say, "I don't want to waste my time, and I don't want to waste your time and money. Read this book. If there's something there that interests you, give me a ring and make an appointment and come and see me again."

Do you know what the interview between Alexander and a prospective pupil actually involved?

I do. In fact, I saw FM do it many a time, because I'd often be in Ethel Webb's room and see what was going on through the open door. I should emphasise that FM was always very friendly with new people and was very good at putting them at their ease. He'd say, "Now, come and sit down in the chair." And he'd allow them to sit down by themselves, although of course he'd notice what they were doing as they did so. Then he'd ask them to stand up again. This gave him a beginning, somewhere to start – and he would go on to explain that he wasn't going to teach them what to do right, but that together they would find out what was going wrong and creating misuse. He'd say: "Now, you're doing yourself harm because you've developed certain habits in the way you use your body which are actually destroying it."

But FM didn't place too much of a burden on people at the outset. He was very sensitive to how they were reacting – and, of course, as you can imagine some of them were terrified and very frightened. But then FM would start working with them and that was so interesting, although again I must emphasise that he wouldn't do very much at this stage. As a starter, he just explained that they were to say 'no' to whatever he suggested. Then he would get them to bend their knees in order to arrive on the chair and they would think, "Now, how did that happen?" You see, he wouldn't let them do what they normally did. Of course, it didn't always work but when it did it was often an absolute revelation for the person.

He'd then work on them to get a further change in their back and then say, "Now, I'm going to get you out of the chair, but I want you to say 'no'." Then he would take them out of the chair to standing.

Did he give instructions about the legs?

He would just tell people to put their knees apart. However, everything he did was very adaptable to the individual.

So did Alexander want a commitment from prospective pupils at the interview?

No, not really.

They were free to continue or abandon the enterprise at any time if they felt like it?

Yes, although he normally knew who was going to make it and who wouldn't. Furthermore, if he didn't think the pupil was serious then he wouldn't bother. You see, his time was so precious and he was so busy that he didn't want to waste his energy.

Lessons were very expensive so it's clear that Alexander was giving lessons to British society's elite while he was working at Ashley Place.

FM with the Earl of Lytton (1939)

Yes, the people coming to lessons were usually well-to-do. He used to say, "People don't appreciate what they don't pay for." On the other hand, although he said that, he didn't behave like that. Take me as an example. I had just lost my father and I had no money. I didn't pay a penny for my lessons or for my training, for that matter. If someone was in need and was interested he was there for them.

In fact, I remember there was a boy who used to work in Sainsbury's almost opposite Ashley Place in Victoria Street where FM used to go and buy his food. Now, this boy had the most appalling stammer. FM observed this for quite some time and then thought to himself, "Poor boy, he can hardly get a word out. This must be very difficult for him because he's a shop assistant." So one day when he was in Sainsbury's he said to the boy, "Look, I've got a house just across the road. Would you do me a favour and come and see me one evening. I think

PART 1: SOME HISTORY

we can do something about your stammer." So the boy made an appointment with the secretary and came to see FM, who told him about the work and said that he thought he could help him. The boy had a course of lessons and his stammer went. He was delighted. And so was FM.

I presume that even though Alexander was critical of the term 'posture' in his writings a lot of people would have come for lessons as they do today because they thought it would improve their posture.
Absolutely. But FM explained from the outset that the Technique wasn't about posture or fixed positions but rather the relationship of parts to parts. This reminds me of one particular man who came to an interview with FM – he'd obviously read a lot of FM's books and had got some very funny ideas about what the Technique involved – and when FM walked in he said: "But you look quite normal!" To which FM replied: "What did you expect to see – a monster?" You see, he was a very agile man. In fact, FM was a very good dancer – very loose and free in the joints. Now I know all about the accusation made nowadays that a lot of Alexander people look stiff and rigid but that's all because they will try and do it. - They will put their heads forwards and up, they will try to lengthen themselves and so on, but as we know that's no good.

What level of success did Alexander achieve in getting the message across to pupils? Furthermore, did he have many failures?
On the whole he was very successful. If that hadn't been the

case the work wouldn't have survived – he couldn't have survived. But, of course, he did have his failures because, as the old saying goes, and as with any learning process, you can take a horse to water but you can't make it drink. And there are some people who really are unteachable – they want you to do all the work and not lift a finger at any time. And we must always keep in mind that what distinguishes the Technique from other disciplines is that it's a re-educational process. The pupil has to become aware of what it is that he or she is doing, and find out what's wrong in order not to carry on doing it.

But generally FM was very good at getting the message across. Indeed, he would point out to people how they were misusing themselves – for example, how they were making so much tension by pressing down into the floor as they were walking – and he would demonstrate and show them the difference between their habitual way of moving and a new way. Really, this is the magical thing about the Technique if it's properly taught. The teacher doesn't merely point out to someone what's wrong, but instead shows them how to prevent it happening. In a way it's predictive. In effect, a teacher is saying to the pupil: "If you do this, this and this, then this will be the outcome. However, if you approach the matter with a bit of intelligence using inhibition and the relevant directions you can achieve a different outcome which will be of lasting benefit to you."

Nevertheless, I assume that there must have been any number of people who were eager to learn the Technique but who would have said to Alexander (as

they say to their teachers today): "Now, that's all very nice. It works beautifully while I'm here in the teaching room and while you're helping me. But what about applying this to real life – how am I going to do that?"

Indeed. But FM encouraged them to work on themselves when he wasn't there. And, of course, after a few lessons he would make suggestions to them like, "Now, when you get ready for bed tonight I want you to go about your business very slowly. When you're doing your teeth, taking your clothes off, and all the other things you've got to do I want you to go much more slowly than you are used to and give your orders all the time. Then when you get into bed, I want you to start off by lying on your back with your knees up as long as it's not too draughty. Lie there for a while and give your orders before turning over and settling down. Don't have too many pillows. Just lie on your side and make sure that the space between your head and the bed is filled.

"Then first thing in the morning when you wake up, don't leap out of bed otherwise it will be 11 o'clock before you even think about freeing your neck. Stay there for a while with the knees drawn up and give your orders. Then get out of bed slowly – don't rush it. It's not good for you to go from lying on your back for hours and then to spring out of bed. Then you can work out the times in the day when it's easy for you to think about inhibiting and directing. I don't expect you to think about it all day long – nobody can. But if you link up thinking about inhibiting and directing, say, when you stop for a meal and you're not under any time pressure then you're on your way – you're off to a good start. Gradually you can expand your repertoire to other times during the day."

He was very practical, you see. For example, as training course students he used to tell us that if we were waiting for a bus and it was a long time coming, or if we were caught in a traffic jam there was no point in getting upset about it. He would say: "Don't get angry, give your orders instead. In that way, you can begin to extend the Technique to your emotional reactions."

When and how did Alexander hit upon the idea of using the chair as a method of teaching the Technique?

Well, that was fairly early on when he had his mirrors rigged up and he was observing himself in speaking and various other activities. While he was doing this he was standing for the most part. But he didn't stand all the time – he obviously sat down at intervals to have a rest.

Presumably, he saw that the interference he observed while he was reciting was also there in the head and neck as he went to sit.

Exactly. When he went to sit he obviously thought, "Oh, my God! Look at what I'm doing to myself!" So that's how using the chair in teaching came about in his life. For pupils, he simply explained that the chair was a very useful vehicle for learning – it's something that in our culture we're doing all day long. He'd say, "If I can teach you how to avoid those habits in this simple activity, you'll be able to extend it to other areas of your life – even to your emotional reactions, which is the hardest task of all."

PART 1: SOME HISTORY

But, of course, he fully appreciated how difficult it was to develop sufficient energy to pay attention to what you're doing with yourself for a lot of the day. A lot of time people will be distracted by one thing and another – they have jobs to do and so on.

But from what you've said, Alexander was keen that his pupils punctuated the day with episodes of thinking about inhibition and directing – getting in and out of bed, getting in and out of the chair, meal times and so on.
Yes. As I've said previously, FM was a very practical man. And although a lot of people got the wrong end of the stick, he always emphasised that this work wasn't about getting in and out of chairs.

It's about paying attention to how you're using your body whatever you're doing – even standing on your head if that's what you want to do!

Did Alexander cut short a course of lessons with a pupil if he thought that they weren't going anywhere – in other words, if he was unable to detect any progress?
Yes. He'd say, "I'm sorry but I don't think I'm going to be able to help you." And he used to say to us: "There are certain types of people – I call them vampires – and you've got to be able to spot them and get rid of them otherwise they'll suck the blood out of you. They won't do any work." And it's true. If you find at the end of the lesson that you're exhausted instead of being rather stimulated, have a look at that person. You shouldn't be exhausted. It's a two-way thing between teachers and pupils.

I've certainly never forgotten FM's warning, and it has stood me in good stead over the years.

But surely this is all relative. A feeling of fatigue or tiredness will change according to the experience of the teacher. For example when someone first starts teaching there will always be people who will tire them out, but over time that won't necessarily be the case.

That's quite true. The pupil will alter and you will alter over time. I fully agree with you. Nevertheless, when you're teaching you are trying to get the person to become responsible for themselves – to learn how to inhibit and give orders. But there are some people whom you can't get to do that. They don't want that. What they want is for you to do it all for them. They like to come along and lie on your couch and have a lovely time and not do any work until they come at the same time next week.

My analogy of the Alexander situation is with a piano pupil. He or she has a lesson from a teacher but there's not even a piano in the house where the student lives so there is no opportunity to practise. So next week the student goes back to the teacher without anything going on in the meantime and – lo and behold – nothing's happened. Nothing's been learned. It's clear that no matter how brilliant the teacher may be, the pupil will never improve. Having said that, in my experience of teaching over many years there aren't too many people like that.

Part 2: Alexander's First Training Course

Of course, the training was all very experimental with the first lot of trainees. Certainly there were times when some people got fed up, but I loved every minute of it. And we did try to help each other.

Part 2:
Alexander's First Training Course

When and why was the first training course set up?

It was established after many years of a lot of pressure from a lot of people. You see, FM didn't want to start training young people until he saw that there was a possibility of earning a living from teaching. But there came a time when the work was booming. So many people, like Dr Peter Macdonald, Pat Macdonald's father, were saying: "Look, FM, this is all going to die with you if you are not careful. It's time to start training teachers."

So the training course opened in 1931, and the initial plan was for it to run for three years. However, everyone on it except Marjorie Barstow, who had to go back to America to help her father in the family business, had to do an extra year because FM didn't think that the students were ready.

Prior to this, of course, Alexander had really only worked with individuals. How did the training course work?

FM had chosen to work with a single pupil after working in

Australia with a group of drama students. It was after this experience that he realised that individual attention was the only way to do it – in other words, he realised how difficult it is to understand the work in a group setting and he gave up trying to teach it in that way. On the other hand, he did do group work with the children who attended the Little School. In fact, Pat Macdonald and I used to go there twice a week after it had moved to Penhill and worked with them in a group as well as individually.

But the point I would like to make is that all of the children at the Little School had had a long course of individual lessons from FM before any work in a group began. And it was the same with people who were on the training course. Everyone had had a lot of lessons with FM before they were allowed to train.

And that's the way it should be. The idea, which has become increasingly fashionable in recent years, that you can take people who haven't had lots of lessons and get them to learn the Technique in a large class is completely ridiculous. If FM couldn't do it in that way, why should we assume that we can? And the danger is that the people who attend these sessions won't have a clue what's going on, and many will dismiss the Technique as ineffectual because they have had a poor experience. In my opinion, teaching introductory classes to groups can only cause great harm to the reputation of the Alexander Technique.

On the training course, even though we were in a group while we were waiting for our turn with FM, the emphasis was that we were meant to work on ourselves by giving a stimulus to move in some way, perhaps going backwards and forwards in the chair, performing a monkey, or whatever we wanted to do. And the whole time, FM was keeping an eagle eye on us.

Of course, the training was all very experimental with the first lot of trainees. Certainly there were times when some people got fed up, but I loved every minute of it. And we did try to help each other. However, because I started a few terms after the others I wasn't allowed to use my hands for what seemed ages. FM used to say to us: "If you use your hands too soon, you'll just incorporate all your bad habits." So what happened when I first attended the training course was that the others used to work on me in the afternoons, until the magic day arrived when FM said I too could start to use my hands. I should add that there was no formal rule about when you could use your hands – it was all down to how FM assessed some-

FM and trainees from the first training course at a party at Penhill (1932)

one's progress. I had to wait a particularly long time because of the state I was in; I had no back to speak of – it was like a piece of string.

And how many hours were you expected to do each day?
It was two hours, never more than that. And it went on being two hours even later on when there were only four of us left, which was wonderful because we all got so much individual attention. Everyone would sit on a chair and FM would go round and give everyone a turn. Then sometimes he'd get us all to sit on a big black couch and watch two of us giving a turn to someone else – one person might put their hands on the head and the other on the back, for example – and those of us who weren't involved would give criticism. The idea behind this was to develop and refine our observational skills. He used to say, "Use your eyes, look at what you're doing."

In fact, he emphasised that we should use everything at our disposal. He said: "You've got to use all your senses in this work." In fact, I've developed something over the years which I call my 'inner ear'. I've learned to listen to my pupil with my inner ear. I developed the use of it quite early on and I think it is very important.

Can you define what you mean by your inner ear?
I suppose it's a quality of attention really. It's why after some years your hands just go to a certain place and the pupil will remark: "How did you know that's the place that's hurting?" In reply I tend to say, "I don't know how I know, but my hands know."

That's very interesting. It raises the question of how Alexander taught the students to use their hands on the training course.

Probably the biggest influence was FM putting his hands over yours when they were on someone. But before he did this he would always lengthen your arms out first and place your hands on, say, someone's head or wherever. Then he would put his hands over yours and you would sense the direction that he was providing.

What did he tell you to think when you had your hands on a fellow student?

Just the guiding orders really. A lot of the teaching was non-verbal, you see. He'd have his hands on yours and you'd get the message. But he was always very insistent that we should start with the head, and then come back to the head after everything else had been worked on. For example, if you took a shoulder, you would always go back to the head. And he was always telling us to keep our eyes on the pupil's neck and head the whole time. He used to say, "It's no good working on something if you're interfering with the back and head. You've got to keep everything going. If you're taking a leg down, for instance, watch the head. If what you're doing or what the person is doing is interfering with the head, stop and then go back to the head."

Over the years, different training courses have devised an enormous number of different ways of teaching students how to put their hands on.

Oh, there was nothing like that. It wasn't painting by numbers or anything of that kind. FM would just ensure that your hands were free. It was more a question of seeing what the situation was and making sure that you reacted appropriately.

What did he tell you regarding the legs?

If you were sitting in a chair you wanted to direct the knees forward from the hips and away from each other in order to get good tone going in the legs. If you were standing the crucial thing was not to bring the knees together.

The primary control is often thought of as an exclusive property of the head-neck-back relationship, but obviously it has a reciprocal relationship with the limbs. How do you see it?

That's absolutely right. When you get the primary control working you have to add on as many orders as you need in whatever activity you are doing. The 'reciprocal relationship' as you put it, is best explained in something like hands on the back of a chair where you have a big, long sequence of orders – it's 'neck free, head forward and up, back to lengthen and widen, knees to go forward from the hips and away from each other; head forward, knees forward, hips back; hold the chair gently but firmly with straight fingers, order the wrists in, pull to the elbows, widen the upper part of the arms as you widen the back.' Which is quite a lot.

Your answer prompts the question: did Alexander teach this level of complexity in the orders to private pupils,

as well as the students on the training course?
Very definitely! Not at the beginning, of course, but most certainly later on after someone had had sufficient lessons.

What information did he give you about the feet?
Well, it depended on what you were doing. Let's take something like monkey. Some people when they put their knees forward from the hips and away from each other will push the ankles out thereby twisting the feet. So if that's a tendency, you want to order the ankles in a bit. Each order through the body is the opposite of the one that went before. The trouble is it's not a type of thinking we're familiar with. We like to go one way or the other, whether it is up or down or whatever.

By and large, we like linear and symmetrical directions rather than the sort of thinking involved in getting what Alexander called the 'antagonistic actions' to work.
Exactly so.

Alexander has quite a detailed section in the 1945 edition of *Man's Supreme Inheritance* where he describes what's involved in the 'acts of sitting and rising from a sitting position.'

In summary form, he says that firstly, the pupil is to 'rid the mind of the idea of sitting down' and to consider the 'means' and not the 'end.'

Secondly, the pupil is instructed to adopt the 'correct standing position, with the back of the legs almost touching the seat of the chair.'

Thirdly, the pupil should give the directive orders involved in getting 'the muscles of the neck to relax' at the same time as allowing 'the head *forward* and up' and fourthly the pupil should think of 'the general idea of the lengthening of the body.'

The fifth stage involves the pupil ordering 'simultaneously the hips to move backwards and the knees to bend' with the 'knees and hip-joints acting as hinges' while also ordering the back to widen.

On reaching the chair, the pupil is then told to 'pause for an instant' and then 'after ordering the neck to relax and the head *forward* and up, the spine to lengthen and the back to widen, come back into the chair' to an upright position by 'using the hips as a hinge, and without shortening the back, stiffening the neck, or throwing up the head.'

Alexander then goes on to say that the 'act of rising is merely a reversal of the foregoing.' The pupil is instructed to 'draw the feet back so that one is slightly under the seat of the chair', allowing the 'body to move forward from the hips' while maintaining the 'freedom of the neck and the idea of lengthening the spine.'

Then the whole body is allowed to come forward so that the centre of gravity 'falls over the feet'. Finally, Alexander instructs the pupil to straighten the 'legs at the hips, knees, and ankles, until the erect position is perfectly attained.'

So an obvious question: was this still customary behaviour on the first training course?

The first thing I'd like to say is that FM's account is all very interesting – indeed, some of the details are still very valuable – but all of this emerged at an earlier part of his teaching career. By the time we were on the training course he'd given up a lot of the stuff he'd written about in earlier editions of *Man's Supreme Inheritance*. He saw that a lot of those instructions were unnecessary, especially the one about the 'correct standing position', which involved putting one foot behind the other before the act of sitting. I think he also found it useful at one stage to highlight drawing the feet back with one slightly under the seat because that attitude provides a little bit of purchase in getting out of the chair.

He'd come to realise that he could get the co-ordination perfectly well with the feet level. I also think that he got much cleverer with his hands as time went on and found that he could drop a lot of these extraneous things because he found he could get what he wanted without them. And, of course, towards the end of his life he said that he could get it independently of the pupil's thinking. It's something that Walter Carrington is always quoting.

But how useful is getting it independently of the pupil's thinking from a learning perspective?

Well, it's no good at all – this is the whole problem! It's why it's so important to establish for the pupil that it's learning from the very first lesson. I think it's crucial for pupils to establish that trust, that if they think something then that thing will happen in the body. It is why, for example, when I've got somebody on the table, I'll sometimes get them to add another order after those to the neck, head and back to release the hip joints. I have my hands on their knees and I wait until the order is carried out. Then I move the legs, and they move like silk.

So, I point this out to the pupil – that I didn't do anything different: the difference occurred in *their* brain and nervous system, which then released *their* hips. It's a very practical demonstration, and the pupil can't get away from the fact that it was their ordering that created the change. Then if you can emphasise to the pupil that they can say, "No", and then give the orders and not try to get it right, they'll come in one day and say something like: "I had an extraordinary experience last night. I went to bed with a headache, and I thought I would give it a try and so I gave my orders and the headache went." Now, that is very definitely not the teacher – that's them. And they will realise that. They will say to themselves: "I did that myself." Of course, it may not be successful every time, but even if it happens a few times the pupil knows that it came from within. In a sense, I am weaning the pupil from that dependency on a teacher from the very first lesson.

Okay, so we have established that Alexander had dispensed with a lot of what he had written earlier in his teaching career about how to get in and out of the chair. How, then, did he instruct the students on the training course about how to take people in and out of the chair?

The idea was to take the pupil straight up and straight down in order to get the back working. There is much more chance of this happening if the pupil is using the legs properly. And I should add that it's very difficult to get the optimum conditions working if the teacher brings the pupil quite a way forward because the tendency is for the lower back to go in – to a greater or lesser extent. Having said that, in some circumstances it might well be appropriate to take someone a little way forward as you take them in and out of the chair. Indeed, sometimes FM would put you in a monkey, get the back working, and then tell you to keep moving the knees so that you would end up in the chair at an angle. Then he would straighten you up so that you were sitting vertically.

But FM always used to emphasise that it's the preparatory work that matters. You can't take someone straight up out of the chair until you've got the head, neck and back working well. When all that's in place, there's normally no problem – it all works very easily, particularly if the pupil is instructed to come back to the teacher's arm. You've only got to watch FM working on the young man and the other people in the short film that's now available to see what I mean.

Sometimes if you were going very, very well FM would just put a hand on the back and take you up – you were meant to look after your own head, in other words. But that was a rarity. In fact, the real skill in using the hands is to learn how to keep the balance between them – for example, when they are placed on the pupil's head. You've got to ensure that there isn't too much back hand, too much front hand, too much thumb or whatever. In fact, using the hands is a very subtle skill, and it takes ages for people to learn how to employ them effectively.

Overall, when you have your hands on a pupil you are endeavouring to the best of your ability to find out what's happening in them. And you soon get the message about whether the head's going back, pulled sideways or what have you. So as a teacher your task is to try to find out the cause of what's going on and then start by undoing the tension in the neck. Really, the only things that can exert traction on the head are the neck muscles – they are in direct contact with the head, and thus the prime cause of any contraction. Then having got a little more freedom there, you give the direction for the head to go forward from the sub-occipital muscles, and as soon as that happens it goes up of its own accord. It does itself, in other words. And it's very important for people to realise that it does not have to be *done* in any way.

If you're working by yourself and you're aware of stiffening of the neck then all you need to do is inhibit at that moment, and then send messages that you hope are going to free the neck, and then direct the head forward and up. It may not work at first but that's all you can do. You keep on projecting the order for the neck to release, and then the head will go forward and up of its own accord.

Really, it's all quite simple: as soon as you stop pulling your head back, what else can it do apart from go forward? But you certainly can't get it by making any sort of movement of the head, although I know that's what a lot of people, including Alexander teachers, try and do. Let me put it another way: you're already making the movement by pulling the head back and down, or over to the side or any of the other variations that are possible. So, you've just got to stop doing that, and the right thing will do itself.

In chair work on the training course, FM would do quite a

lot of preparatory work in standing – 'getting you going' as he used to say – and then move you very easily so you ended up in the chair. Then he would often sit beside you giving you the head direction, working on the back and very often on the shoulders. Sometimes he'd say to us, "shoulders back and down", which is great if it works. But I think that's a very tricky order for people to understand – it almost encourages them to do something. Instead, nowadays I prefer to give a pupil the idea of allowing the shoulders to be part of the back, which is very much an undoing. In fact, all of the Technique is about undoing – that's why we don't have to move the head by nodding or anything like that.

When he was sitting beside you, FM would sometimes also put one hand on the knee and one hand on the back and move your leg. He'd apply quite a lot of pressure, and instinctively because of that you allowed the leg to go out.

Do you think that there is any advantage (as Frank Pierce Jones suggests in his book, *Freedom to Change*) in asking the pupil or student to become aware of the pressure of the head against the hand of the teacher in order to highlight any distortion in the neck-head-back relationship?

I have no quarrel with that. What I might do in the situation where someone is really pushing back is say, "Now, you're pressing your head into my hand. Do it a bit harder." It's just an extrapolation from one of the magical things that FM used to tell us to do if we had someone lying on the couch and they were pressing their head back into the books. He suggested that if you'd tried everything else to prevent someone pulling back the head you should say: "Now, go on do it as hard as you can. And stop. Now do it again. And stop." That way they soon get the message.

That's very intriguing. What other instructions or information did Alexander provide you with concerning lying down work?

We spent hour after hour learning to take a leg without shoving it up into the hip joint, and to allow the back to lengthen and widen and so on. However, FM always used to emphasise how important it was to get the pupil not to help you, say, with the legs and arms. So he put a great deal of emphasis on getting the pupil to inhibit while he or she was lying down.

Presumably he gave you specific instructions about how to take a shoulder and so on.

Yes, FM would get us to put the hand under the shoulder blade with the other hand on top and encourage it to widen out. As I said, at first he told us to give the pupil the order 'shoulder back and down' because everyone tends to lift and round them. However, later on in the training course he stopped using those words when he realised that despite the emphasis on inhibition nearly everyone tries to do it. FM was very clever that way. When he found that a form of words led to people doing something he hadn't originally meant or intended, he stopped using them.

I notice that you don't apply any pressure – for

example, by using your body weight – when you are taking the shoulder out.
No, I don't. Everyone clenches in the armpit and that's where the primary distortion of the shoulders begins – it doesn't begin somewhere else and end up there, but actually starts there. Really, this is a discovery I've made in the last ten years or so. I tell people to release in the area where I tend to put my thumb – right up in the armpit. And it's very magical when it works. And I often tell a pupil the story of the Zen master, who when he was learning to be a monk, was told to imagine that he had a raw egg under each armpit in order to stop any undue tightening. It goes to show that other traditions know something about the harm that clenching in the armpit does.

How about when someone is on the couch and you provide some gentle pressure to the knees?
That's very useful. In fact, I always get the person to think about the back widening and then try to get the undoing. I make it clear to the pupil what I'm trying to do so that it's not an overly mysterious process.

Did Alexander give you any indication or guidance about how long you were meant to work with a pupil in lying down either on the floor or the table?
Not really. He left it to us to work out. Everyone's different. Take someone with a really terrible back. Obviously, it's better to do a little bit of work in the chair first and then put them down for a longer period than someone who doesn't have the same problem. I find nowadays, working mainly with teachers and

LYING DOWN WORK

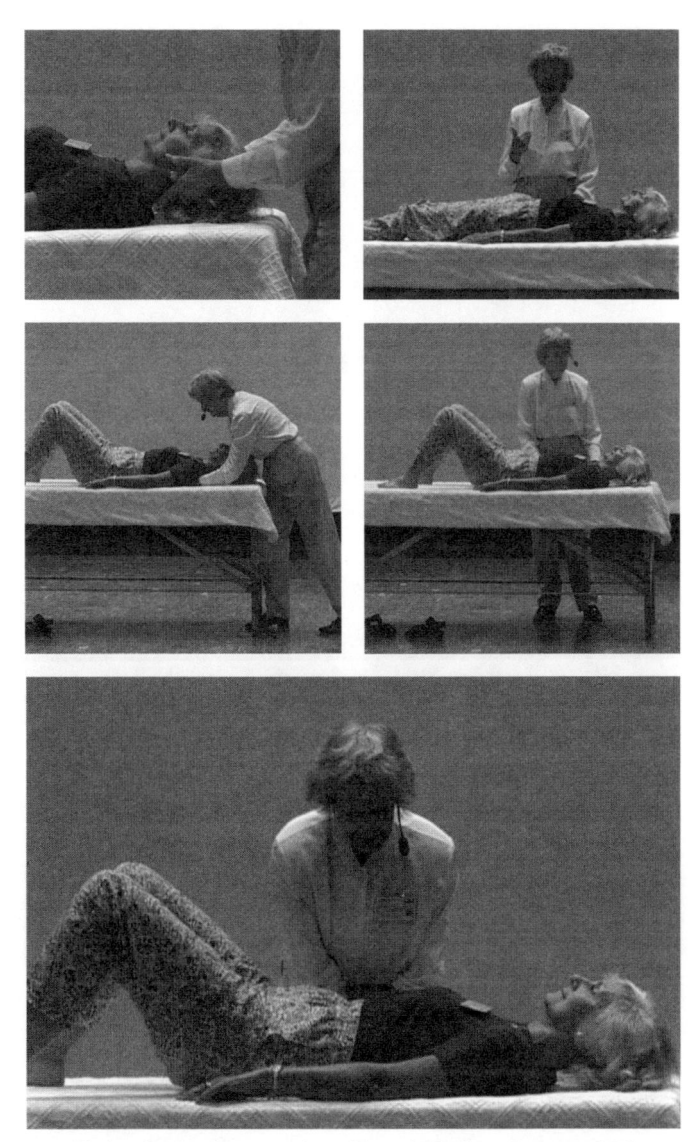

Marjory Barlow demonstrating table work (Freiburg Congress 1999)

PART 2: ALEXANDER'S FIRST TRAINING COURSE

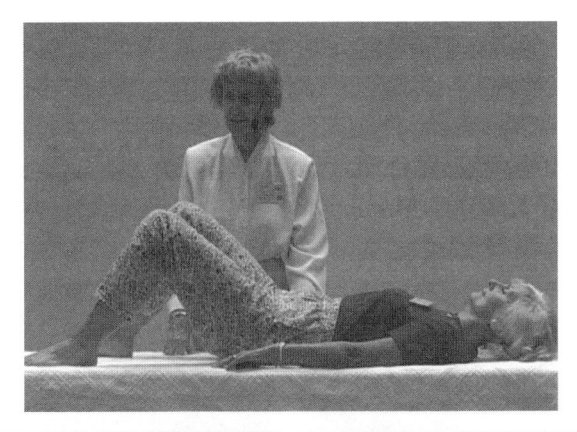

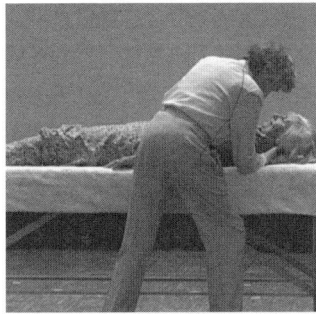

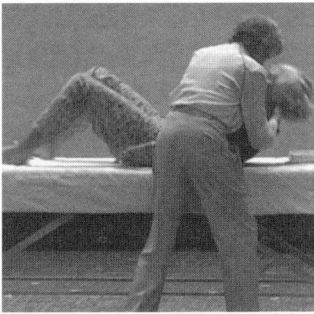

Marjory Barlow moving a pupil from lying to sitting (Freiburg Congress 1999)

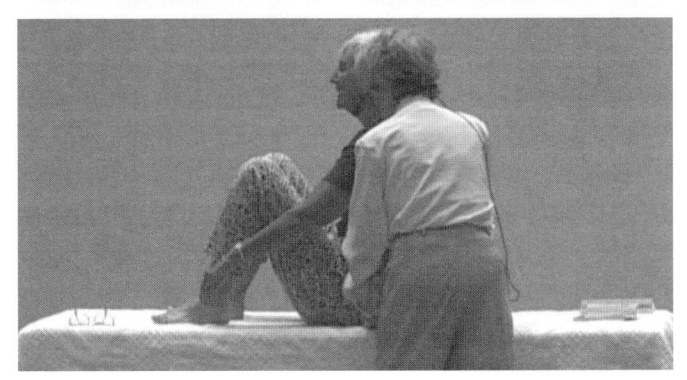

students, that they're all so tired, and so I give them quite a lot of lying down work.

However, Alexander didn't do much lying down work with his pupils.

That's right. From the beginning he delegated that to his assistants. But if we were giving a pupil or fellow student lying down work and we were in trouble or experiencing difficulty, he would come along and help us.

But there was a golden rule: he said that if you are taking a leg or some other part of the body, you should watch the neck and head. If the pupil reacts to what you are doing by pulling down, you're destroying the whole process. If that happened, FM would tell us to put the leg down again and go back to the head.

Nowadays when I am working on someone, then between every single thing I do, I go back to the neck and head. And I've also got my eye on that area all the time I'm working somewhere else. And, of course, you have to remind the pupil not to interfere with the neck and head. Really, every problem that we have been discussing is a failure of inhibition. Often the pupil is bothering about something other than their head and neck – they're trying to help or not to help and all the variations that go with it.

You're trying to bring the inhibitory process to the foreground of the pupil's awareness, in other words.

That's right. It's basic, you see. Nothing has any value without inhibition.

PART 2: ALEXANDER'S FIRST TRAINING COURSE

Using the floor in teaching is different in some interesting respects from using a table. For example, in taking a pupil's head while they are lying on the floor the teacher's arms will often be at a different angle and are straighter than when using a table.

You're quite right. That's a very good bit of observation. But whether I'm using the floor or the table the orders I'm giving are: "Wrist in, pull to the elbow, widen the upper part of the arm as I widen the back." That's true for most things really.

You're not a fan of a teacher giving a pupil a lesson while sitting on the floor, however. Can you explain why?

I would much prefer it if a teacher went into a squat, which is the way FM taught us to do it. I know that a squat is jolly hard work, but because you are getting the antagonistic pulls to work, the experience for the pupil is so much better.

Did Alexander encourage the students in any way – indeed, did you or anyone else find any need or have the desire – to create new ways of working on the training course?

We were so busy trying to get on with the ones he'd given us I don't think we had time. I mean when you think of it we had getting into the chair and getting out of the chair, moving backwards and forwards in the chair, going into monkey, putting hands over the back of the chair in sitting or standing, the whispered ah, going on your toes, using the wall and so on. And you have to remember also that we were encouraged to combine things like, for example, performing the whispered ah as you moved backwards and forwards in the chair. Another one FM liked us to do was to go up on to the toes with hands over the back of the chair.

So there was plenty to do on the training course. There was no need to manufacture or invent anything else.

Did you have a favourite activity?

Of all the different things FM got us to do, I always found going on the toes very interesting because in performing it you have to go against what feels possible.

Do you know anything about the origins of going up on to the toes?

I know that he taught it when he was giving lessons in Australia. For example, my mother, who was ten years younger than FM, twice fell off a swing and injured her hip when FM was away teaching in New Zealand, which would have been some time in the mid 1890s. Now the orthopaedic people wanted to 'scrape the bone' as she put it. However, when he heard this, FM came rushing back before any surgery could be performed and started working on my mother. And one of the things he got her to do was to stand with her fingertips on the mantelpiece and then go up and down on her toes. She said it used to drive her mad. But there's no doubt that it cured her hip problem.

Why did Alexander instruct your mother to put the fingertips on the mantelpiece?

That was just to give her that little bit of support so that she wouldn't throw the body forward – you know that awful swing forward that we all tend to do when faced with the situation of going up on to the toes. It helped her stay back, in other words.

The students on the first training course were also involved in various drama productions. How did that come about?

Well, FM had already done this when he was teaching in Australia. For us, he used the plays to demonstrate a number of things. First, he wanted to ensure that we wouldn't suffer from stage fright. Secondly, that we would be heard in every seat in the theatre, which wasn't at all easy in Sadler's Wells or the Old Vic because both venues had 'empty' spots. And the third reason was that he wanted us to use ourselves well throughout the performance – unless, of course, you were playing a part like Old Gobbo, the blind widower, in *The Merchant of Venice*.

But what was so brilliant, was that FM wouldn't allow us to learn the parts. We used to rehearse by taking it in turns – it didn't matter whether you were male or female – to take all the different roles, and read the relevant parts of the play.

If we were reading it in such a way that it was clear we didn't understand a word of what we were saying, we would stop. He really wanted us to understand what the words meant. In fact, we took a whole year working on *The Merchant of Venice*. Personally, I learned so much from the experience about how to help people on stage and, indeed, performers generally.

And FM got Matheson Lang, who was a pupil of his and a very well-known actor, to come in and cast us. Some parts were obvious but others less so. I ended up being cast as Nerissa, which is a lovely part. In *Hamlet*, the following year, I played Horatio – we were short of men – and everyone said I looked like the principal boy in pantomime, but it was so wonderful because I had these scenes playing opposite FM.

Was Alexander a good actor?

Oh yes. He was a much more expressive actor than was the fashion at the time when you didn't emote or do anything very much. But, of course he'd worked with and watched people like Sir Henry Irving and Viola Tree after he'd come to England. By observing them he learned so much. I think he was very, very good. And it really is astonishing that a man of his age could play Hamlet so successfully. It was quite something really.

You obviously enjoyed it, but how about everyone else?

You've read Lulie Westfeldt on the subject?

Yes. She wasn't exactly bowled over by the experience.

But you can understand it in her case. No matter how much she'd changed, because of the effects of the polio she had as a child, she was still deformed to a certain extent. And it was a great ordeal for her to go on the stage. In fact, she played the judge in the trial scene of *The Merchant of Venice* and absolutely hated it. I also think a lot of the other students thought that acting was a complete waste of time. They didn't really understand the value of it for our future careers. On the other hand, despite what Lulie says in her book, we all had a lot of fun with it.

Certainly, Patrick Macdonald enjoyed it – he played

Gratiano in *The Merchant of Venice* although I can't recall what role he played in *Hamlet*.

Nevertheless, whatever its merits Alexander dropped the theatrical experience from the curriculum. Do you know why?

I don't know for sure – I never asked him why he stopped. My guess is that he realised there was too much grumbling amongst the students!

And you mentioned that he extended the training course by a year for your intake.

He did for the others but not for me as I hadn't started the training until 1933. But I know that FM thought that the students weren't ready so he decided to add the next year although he didn't charge any extra for this. However, by the end of his life he was saying that a training course should be six years in duration. I think we've got to face the fact that it's a lifetime's learning in many ways.

In my final year, as I mentioned previously, there were only four of us, which was absolutely wonderful. When there were twelve people on the training course, it wasn't so easy to pin FM down in quite the same way as when there were fewer of us. And the great thing was that we still had him for two hours a day. So it was much easier to say: "FM, you're making too big a leap there. Could you go back and take some smaller steps so that we can understand a bit more clearly."

I think one of the problems was that he saw it all so quickly, and we often couldn't follow him very well. But challenging him in the way I have indicated meant that we got more explanation and clarification than some of the other students who had already qualified.

Over what period did you continue to work on the training course?

I worked right up until the time FM left for America in 1941. He asked me to carry on the training with all the people who hadn't been called up, which was quite a small group. I carried on until Ashley Place was bombed, which happened in November. All the windows were blown in, and the front steps were all broken. There was also a big hole in the road outside the building.

The training course resumed in 1943 when FM returned to London. He asked me to come in and help him. However, by then I had two small children so I had to get a nanny. For a while I worked between ten o'clock in the morning and four o'clock in the afternoon. But it was all too much. I felt I had to be with my children, so after six months I said to FM that I would have to withdraw and just give private lessons at home. He was very understanding.

Because you worked as an assistant to Alexander over a number of years you must have seen how the training course evolved. What were the main changes?

Well, each training course was slightly different because of the different personalities on it. I think that although in many ways the basic training remained the same, after the first course FM didn't give so much detailed explanation of things like lying down work. Also, later on he didn't do much work using the wall. In fact, some people came to think that my husband, Bill, had invented it. But he didn't – it was all FM.

I think one element that remained consistent throughout the years I was assisting on the training course was the emphasis FM placed on working by yourself. In other words, we weren't just sitting around waiting for someone's hands to turn up. Instead, we were giving ourselves a stimulus to move a lot of the time. Perhaps I should explain that FM made it very clear to all of the students that they weren't just supposed to sit there and hope that something might happen. Indeed, there was much more chance of something positive happening if you gave yourself a stimulus to move, inhibited it, went through all the orders, and then moved.

Could you say a bit more about that?

Well, let's suppose you're sitting in a chair and you're a bit pulled down. In this sort of situation it's a good idea to give yourself a stimulus to move – backwards or forwards or whatever – then taking your time to inhibit and get the orders going and then perform the movement. You'll find that in the process of moving you will come up out of the pulling down if the messages are getting through. In fact, FM used to demonstrate it for us. He'd sit in a chair and pull himself right down, and then give himself a stimulus to come forward by little stages. By the time he was all the way forward, he was really up. Now that's a very useful thing to learn, although somewhere along the line it's got lost. But it is the very best way for students on training courses to work on themselves.

That's very interesting about the role of movement because I think there's a fairly widespread confusion in the Alexander world about whether you can or should generate improvement in use from a 'static' place.

That's right. FM used to say that the danger of a static position is that you're trying to feel it out rather than letting the messages carry you to somewhere different, which they will do if you allow them to.

You mentioned earlier about Alexander telling you to spend your time usefully if, for example, you are waiting for a bus that hasn't turned up. So stepping outside the rarefied atmosphere of the training course, there you are waiting for the 55, and you become aware that you are doing something inappropriate with your knees – perhaps you're locking them, or some such thing. How to proceed?

Well, you always come back to your neck, head and back and get that going first. Then you give the order to release the knees. But in my case it would depend on how much I felt I was pushing them back. If I was doing it a lot, I would actually make a little movement of them forwards from the hips and away from each other.

Finally, how would you sum up the elements that make up the training of teachers in the Alexander Technique?

What I would really like to emphasise is that all of the things taught on our training course evolved out of a need – initially, the needs of F Matthias Alexander, which he then realised had general relevance. A lot of people nowadays think they're superfluous and want to trade them in for something different. In many ways this seems to be just the pursuit of novelty for novelty's sake. But I say, why throw things away that have been worked out over many, many years? And they are so practical. Every time you clean your teeth or wash your face it's an opportunity to go into monkey. Every time you're in the kitchen making a sauce or gravy and you're stirring it, you should be in a little monkey too. It's all very obvious and sensible when you think about it.

Part 3:
The Ground Rules

One day after the training course class, I was going particularly well and I was sitting in FM's chair and just giving my orders and then after ten minutes or so I just floated up. It was an extraordinary experience, and one that I've never forgotten.

Part 3:
The Ground Rules

Going up on to the toes

Everybody goes up on to the toes by throwing the body forward instead of going straight up. In order to prevent this, FM would take you on to the toes by first getting you going, and then standing behind you with the hands around the lower part of the chest. At that point he would ask you to come back to his hands. He would say, "Now, I'm going to push you forward, and I want you not to let me do that. I don't want you to go forward." So then he would make a gentle pressure to take you forward. And then if you kept coming back you would just pop up and the whole thing would work beautifully.

But he wouldn't try to lift you which is the common mistake that nearly everyone makes nowadays. And, of course, if you are in a good state only a little pressure from the teacher is necessary to take you up.

How long would Alexander keep you on the toes for?

With FM you'd stay up there just a few seconds. Then he'd say,

GOING UP ON TO THE TOES

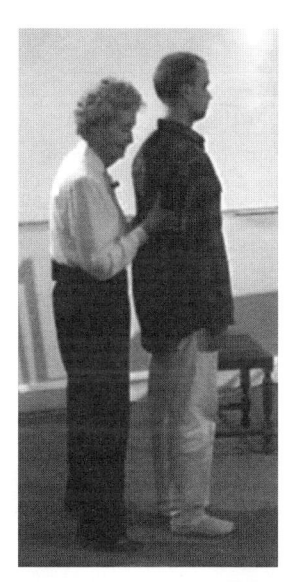

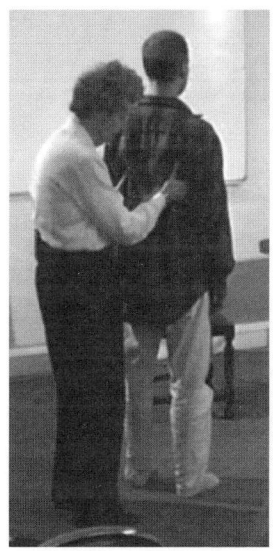

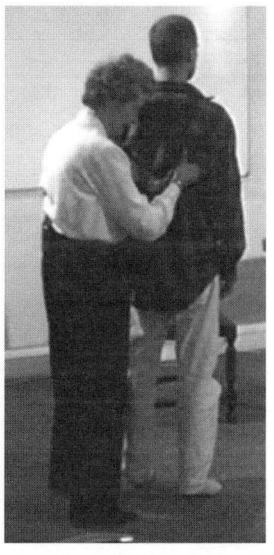

Marjory Barlow teaching going up on to the toes (Regent's College 1998)

PART 3: THE GROUND RULES

"Now release the ankles and don't lose stature." Then down you would come to quite a different place and the whole thing would be organised differently – I don't mean spatially but something had changed throughout the whole body including the feet.

At that point, FM would also often say, "Now, go on with that as if you were going to go on to the toes" – that means not throwing the body forward – "but put your knees forward and away." And then he would take you into monkey. Once you were in monkey, he might also take you on to the toes.

If you were performing going on to the toes by yourself, FM would allow you to put the fingertips on the back of a chair just to give you a bit of moral support. As anyone who has tried it will know, it is very hard to maintain that idea of going back against the feeling that you've got to come forward. But you know that the end is to go on to the toes, and you know you're not going to allow yourself to do what you feel you must do to get on to the toes. If you are clear about your intention, you can then spend ten minutes just standing there giving your orders without much happening. Then all of a sudden up you go! You can then repeat the process if you want.

Going back from the ankles

One important element in this was that FM was very aware of our tendency to throw the body forward all the time. And as I have said previously, he was always telling us how to use our time constructively. For example, you're waiting for a bus, and it's late. "Now, there's no point getting frustrated," he used to tell us. "Do a bit of work instead."

And a very good way to work is to give your orders and come back a tiny fraction from the ankles, give the orders again and come back another tiny fraction. In that way you are giving lots of orders and then making a series of tiny movements. It makes your whole back work. And the interesting discovery that we the students made was that the tinier the fraction you came back from the ankles the more effective it was. Now, by the time you've done that for ten minutes or however long the bus took to arrive, your back could often be quite transformed. Then when the bus came along and you were ready to board, you'd 'try to keep your length' as FM put it.

However, if someone is standing with the head pulled back this isn't going to do a great deal of good, is it? In other words, you need to be in a reasonable state of balance to derive an advantage from it.

Yes, you're right. Going back from the ankles as taught by FM implies that your head is going forwards and up and your back is lengthening and widening. You're giving those orders as primary orders before you even attempt to go back from the ankles.

So if someone is seriously pulling down, how to proceed?

You would direct for quite some time. And probably the bus would have arrived by then!

FM walking in a field

Walking

Irene Tasker had some nice advice about walking. When I was working with her at Ashley Place before I went on the training course she told me that as you walk forward, you should think that your whole back is going in the direction from which you have come. It's a preventative, and it stops you throwing the body forward. It's wonderful – I think everyone should try it!

FM would sometimes walk a pupil at the end of the lesson. He'd say, "Up to put the foot down because we all think down to put the foot down." That was his shorthand version of what was involved. One other thing I should mention is that in preparation for walking FM would stand behind you and give you the widening, and not let you shift the weight from side to side as you initiated the movement forward.

Did he say to come back to his hands?

Yes, he would if you had a tendency to throw the whole trunk forward as you went to move. He'd say: "It's like going on to your toes. Come back."

In this activity and others like it, a big problem for a lot of people is that as they come back from the ankles the toes will lift off the floor.

Yes. It's the tension, isn't it? It's usually caused by stiffening the knees. If there's a problem, the safe thing to do is always go a bit higher. If it's something in the toe, look at the ankle, knee or hips. Always go higher – the problem is usually coming from higher up.

PART 3: THE GROUND RULES

Monkey

I think the term 'monkey' started with the students on the training course. Then FM took it up because he thought it was funny, and because he could see why it was monkey. However, FM always said: "When you go down into monkey always take two bites of the cherry, but when you come up out of it you can do it all in one." He never taught going into it in one movement because he said that was too difficult.

FM used to say that if you were in a bad way then if you inhibited and gave your orders things would improve. So you want to get yourself a little bit organised before starting. The feet are placed hip width apart with the toes turned out slightly which facilitates the knees going forward from the hips and away from each other. Both these things just make going into the monkey that little bit easier. If the feet are too straight, for example, it is very hard to get the knees going away without distorting the ankle. And, of course, if the monkey you are about to perform is going to take you into a deep squat it's a good idea to exaggerate the turn-out of the feet. It is also an advantage to have the legs a little further apart.

So the first stage is to bend the knees – you can bend them a small way or a long way and you can modify it if you like – and you get them going forward from the hip and away from each other whilst maintaining stature as much as you can. In other words, you bend the knees without coming down in space. Of course, I should add that you are meant to maintain your stature as much as you can in whatever you are doing. But the danger point in monkey is when you go forward from the hips – it's very difficult not to pull the back in. So the big thing to look out for in coming forward from the hips is not to allow the knees to come back, which is a very common error.

Ideally, you should be able to perform the movement forward from the hips without any movement in the knees. However, as a preventative, if you have difficulty in this you can also let the knees go forward a little more as you let the head lead and the back lengthen as you move. Performed with

FM in lunge taking Debbie Caplan into monkey (Boston 1941)

PART 3: THE GROUND RULES

direction, this makes it less likely that you will pull the legs into your body.

Once you are in monkey the orders FM used to give us were, "Neck free, head forward, knees forward, hips back – one against the other like a three-way stretch with the head just winning." He would often put his hand halfway down your back and say, "Head forward from there," meaning the middle of the back, "hips back from there and the knees forward." The hand was on that part of the back to get the head going forward and the upper back forward, which again is a preventative as the rest of the back goes back counteracted by the knees going forward from the hips and away from each other.

The position of the head, legs and back doesn't matter – it's the relationship of part to part that's important. The main thing is to ensure that you keep the whole thing free, particularly at the hip, knee and ankle joints. The arms then can just be left to hang freely.

When FM had got you going in monkey, he would often encourage you to perform a whispered ah, which involved a lot of sustained ordering.

The main problem once you're in monkey is that you can start to lose the head, and begin to pull down into the chest. The result is that you begin to fix the joints.

'Head going forward and upper back forward' is interesting. Can you say a bit more about that?

Yes, the order FM gave was to stop you pushing back with the upper back, which is universal. Everyone has that tendency, and we all know that you never want to go with the tendency!

It might also be useful if you said something about the hips going back.

This is often a source of confusion. The pelvis comes up quite far but the hips are where the leg joins the body – it's where the teacher puts a hand to get the direction going at the front of the pelvic bone.

How long did Alexander get you to stay there for?

There were no rules really about how long you should stay in a monkey. In the beginning, you went on until you felt a bit uncomfortable and achy – something would begin to hurt in your back, neck or shoulder or wherever. Then it was time to come up.

To come up, FM said you can do it all in one. You give your orders, straighten your knees and come back from the forward attitude you're in while being careful not to brace the knees.

PART 3: THE GROUND RULES

Squatting

FM used to say that man's worst invention was the chair. In the old days, and still today in many cultures, people either squatted or sat cross-legged on the floor. He used to say that one of the best ways of getting over the problem of being dominated by the chair and sitting is to pretend that it isn't there and behave as if you were going into a deep squat. If you perform it this way you'll eventually hit the chair.

So you organise yourself as if you were going into monkey with the feet turned out, but in this case you have a wider base. If your feet are facing straight forward, then as you put your knees away you've got to twist your ankles, whereas if the feet are well apart then your knees will go forward from the hips and away from each other without any problem.

Initially, you go down as straight as you can and then at a certain point you have to come forward a bit from the hips – in other words, you can go pretty straight but not straight all the way down. And if you were having a problem with flexibility, FM would say: "Now, if you can't get down there, get as far as you can and then come up. Gradually, you can increase the amount you go down." I should add that this meant over time, not at one session. In fact, one of his favourite phrases was "Never force yourself", which I think speaks for itself.

To come up, you have to keep letting your head go forward and up, and you've got to put your knees even further apart – both before you come up and as you're coming up. That's how you get good tone in the legs, which unfortunately very few people possess nowadays.

FM in a squat by a birdcage

Did Alexander teach squatting to pupils as well as the students on the training course?

He used to show it to some of his pupils, but it was really us, the students, who he really showed it to. He had to because we were all working on each other on the floor. And certainly, as we've discussed before, there was no question of sitting on the floor and working on somebody. I would say it's almost impossible to do that and maintain good use. Rather than being a position of mechanical advantage, it would be what FM would call a position of mechanical disadvantage. When we were working on each other we always had to go into a deep squat, or if we were working on a fellow student's legs and taking them up and down, we would go down on one knee.

I presume that you weren't taught this on Alexander's training course, so what do you make of the innovation of squatting using door handles and leaning back before allowing the knees to go forward from the hips and away from each other?

No, we did not do that with FM. But it is very nice. And it resembles and is perfectly consistent with something we did on the training course where you'd have someone lying on the floor, and you would stand near their feet and then take their hands while walking backwards to help them up. It's the same thing really.

The Lunge

FM showed us how to perform this activity on the training course. He didn't actually give it a name – it was Pat Macdonald who called it 'the lunge', and the name sort of stuck.

To start off, you stand quite normally, feet not too far apart, and give your orders. Then while you maintain lengthening of the stature you place one foot in the instep of the other so that the feet are at an angle of 45° or so. You then swivel, turning the

FM working in lunge (Boston 1941)

whole body in that direction. At this point you can let the head lead and pick up the out-turned leg and take a step – it doesn't have to be a big step, a little one will do. You are then supported mainly by the front leg, while the back leg remains straight. You also need to be careful not to brace back the knee.

To come back, you keep your orders going, especially to the neck, head and back and just allow yourself to make the return journey. You can then go into lunge once again and play around with moving the weight between the front and back foot.

I find that it's an activity that is very useful in all kinds of situations. I use it a lot when I'm working with someone on the couch, for example. But it's also very applicable to any number of activities from making a bed to using a vacuum cleaner. It is also very useful when you go to pick something up.

Using the chair in sitting and standing

As I said previously, if FM was working on you, he would take you straight down into the chair. You see, it's very difficult to get your lower back working properly if you go forward from the hips. But if the pupil is coming back as the knees bend, it is much more efficient and effective. However, FM would sometimes take you into monkey first before sitting which is a different thing altogether.

But when you're on your own and you're standing in front of the chair, you need to get everything going and then you actually move your knees forward from the hips and away from each other. The only thing that can bring you down from standing is increased bending of the knees – that's logical, isn't it?

What instructions did Alexander give to his pupils about the legs while sitting?

The most important thing was to allow them to go forward from the hips and away from each other. And the crucial thing is not what position they are in at any given moment, but what electrical impulses you're sending through the nervous system to the legs. For example, sitting with the ankle supported by the opposite thigh is fine. FM used to sit like that when we would go out in the evening. Or you can sit with the legs in front of you with the ankles crossed. But crossing the legs where the thighs are in contact as many people do is very difficult to do without messing everything up. Of course, I'm well aware that there are a couple of pictures of FM sitting on a wall with his

PART 3: THE GROUND RULES

FM seated with pet dog at Penhill

leg crossed over the other one, but if you look at them closely you can see that he is not pulling down in any way.

How about the organisation necessary for when someone moves from sitting to standing?

Before you make the movement, you want to get all the directions going. In effect, what you're doing by giving the orders is comparable to a railway construction where railway lines are put in place so that the train can move along the track. In other words, by giving the orders you're setting everything up so that the movement can take place freely and easily.

If you are quite far back in a low chair it is very difficult to move, and so it's obviously not the best place to start from. In fact, what I always recommend the pupil to do is to move forward a little bit by using the arms to raise the body but not raising the shoulders.

Mostly when people are left to their own devices and decide to move backwards or forwards in the chair they do a sort of shuffle. So FM developed a way to avoid this and, of course, it's also a very good exercise in inhibition and giving orders. In particular, you've got to think about your arms and so on. But whether you're going forwards or backwards in the chair you always put the arms behind you and ideally use the first two knuckles of each hand so that you can get a bit of purchase. The backs of the hands are facing forward with the same sort of directions as the hands over the chair. Now we come to the tricky bit. The important thing to bear in mind is not to raise the shoulders as you raise your body.

I should add that practically none of the teachers who have come to me for lessons in recent years have been taught how to perform this.

That's very interesting. However, the truth is that in a lot of everyday situations people are not in a very co-ordinated state, and yet they still have to move. So once again a real-life situation: you're sitting in the office, a café or wherever and you're slumped. Now it is obvious that you don't want to try to stand up from the slump...

No, that's not a good idea. Because if you're slumping you'll have to throw your body right forward to do it.

PART 3: THE GROUND RULES

How to proceed, then?
Well, you'd have to stop, wouldn't you? You'd then give yourself the stimulus to move a little bit and with some ordering and then some small movements while you remain sitting you would hope to end up in a better place. Then you could stand.

Do you recommend a pupil to come back from the hips before standing?
Yes, I do. In fact, I tend to come back a little bit in order to get my back working. However, if I'm really going well I just have the idea that I'm not going to let the back go forward by thinking the back back and that's enough.

What advice do you have for someone who is sitting at a desk on a conventional chair, who then has to move in order to make the space to be able to stand?
I think the best way is to come forward over the knees, lift the seat of the chair and then move the chair a little way back so that you have some room. Then you can stand up.

So can you sum up what you say to a pupil if you are asked how the type of sitting and standing in a lesson applies to everyday life?
I say, "Well, you don't want to try to stand if you're sitting way back in the chair." I then explain how to move forward using the arms as I explained earlier. Then I emphasise the things that you want to inhibit like throwing the head back and the body forward – let's face it, it's everybody's habit, isn't it? So then I say, "What you have to understand is that you have to get

SITTING AND STANDING

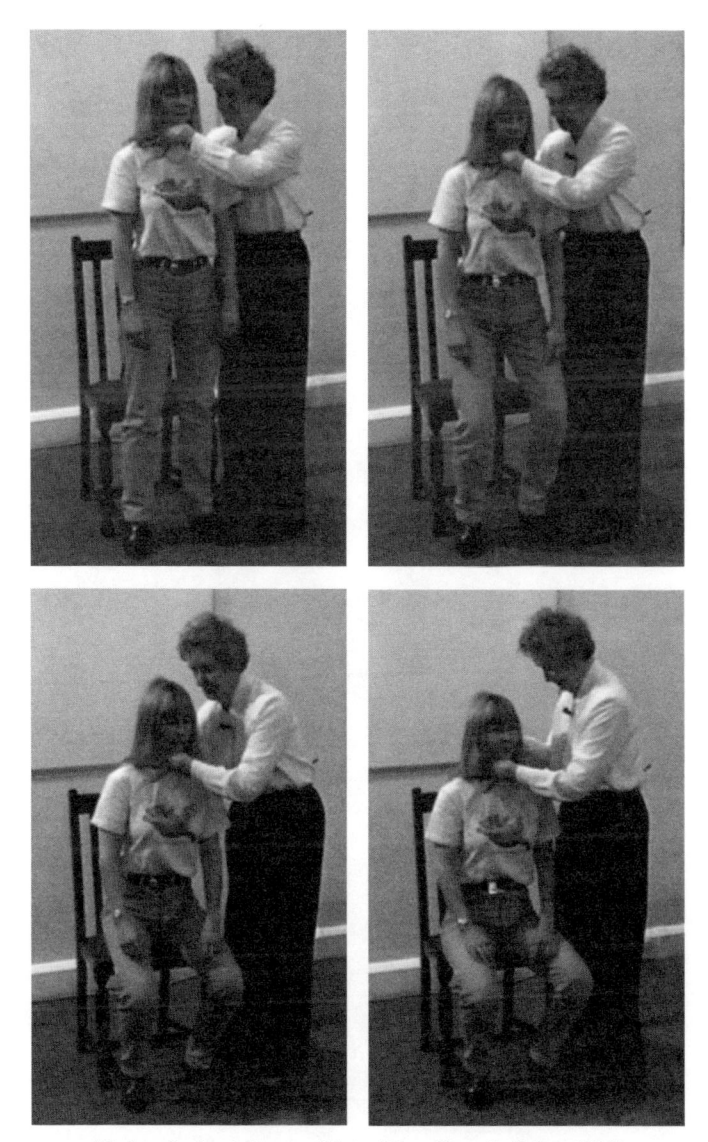

Marjory Barlow taking pupil into sitting (Regent's College 1998)

PART 3: THE GROUND RULES

the head going forward and up, and the back going back as the knees go forward from the hips and away from each other – getting all the contrary pulls in the body working, in other words."

Now, the difficulty most people have is that they will often feel that they can't get out of the chair unless they allow themselves to put the head back and the body forward and contract the legs. But I then explain that it's necessary to overcome that feeling, that they can do it because they know that they can do it with me. And then I tell the story of how one day after the training course class, I was going particularly well and I was sitting in FM's chair and just giving my orders and then after ten minutes or so I just floated up. It was an extraordinary experience, and one that I've never forgotten.

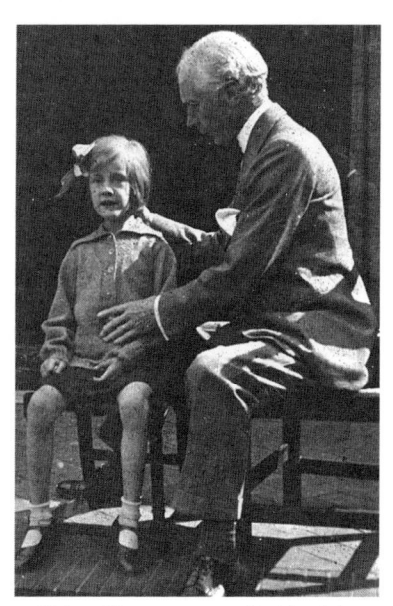

FM teaching a young pupil while sitting

Moving backwards and forwards in the chair

FM would sit in a chair and pull right down, and then give himself a stimulus to move just a fraction and then just another fraction. By the time he'd done this about four or so times he was right up out of himself.

So the lesson behind this is that if you suddenly realise you're pulling down or you're wrong in some way then inhibit, give yourself a stimulus to move a little bit, and then carry on with that until you're in a better shape. As we discussed before, if you want to make an alteration do it in movement rather than trying to do it statically. Keeping still and ordering is fine – you're laying down the pathway – but change is made through movement.

So taking someone to the back of a chair as FM did was an extension of this principle. He wanted to give the pupil an experience that was outside the normal range and in particular an activity where it's very hard not to pull down. However, if you don't stiffen the neck through the movement, you won't 'push the back out of the chair' as he put it.

In *Man's Supreme Inheritance* FM says that you need to place one or two books against the inner back of the chair before inclining the pupil backwards. But that instruction was provided because FM's teaching chair had a hollow in it. And FM would take you a long way back – not from the very front, but certainly when you were seated in the middle of the chair.

As we discussed before, as the pupil comes forward from the back of the chair I get them to put the knees away from each other. It's something I've discovered that helps the pupil,

PART 3: THE GROUND RULES

partly because it gives them something to think about. Like FM and AR, I then sometimes use small movements backwards and forwards from the upright sitting position.

FM taking pupils forward from hips

Hands over the back of a chair

Hands over the back of a chair is something that gradually evolved. I know from talking to FM that when he started teaching full-time he found that by the evening he wasn't able to straighten his arms because of all the work and the tension he had produced in himself. So he had to stop doing whatever it was that he was doing. And hands over the back of a chair is a wonderful basis for using the arms for everything in life. That's why everything FM taught us is still valid – all his procedures are responses to a need. He didn't just invent them for the sake of inventing something.

FM taught hands over the chair to us in both sitting and standing. He never thought one was easier than the other – he never made that kind of distinction. Now he didn't teach it to pupils when they first started lessons, but he did when they had got somewhere with the work. He used to tell us: "Accommodate what you teach them to what they're capable of. Don't give them so much that they get depressed."

For a teacher, if you can do a decent hands over the back of a chair, which requires releasing the shoulders and so forth, you won't come to much harm when you've got a human being in front of you.

I find nowadays that nearly everyone stands much too close to the chair and they don't allow for the length of the arms and, therefore, they end up quite cramped. I should also mention that it doesn't really matter what angle the torso is because, after all, you need different angles for different activities in everyday life. But once you are in monkey the directions are:

PART 3: THE GROUND RULES

'Neck free, head forward and up, back to lengthen and widen, knees to go forward from the hips and away from each other; head forward, knees forward, hips back.' In other words, we are back to FM's three-way stretch. Then with one arm at a time and straight fingers, which you drop from their first joint, gently but firmly take hold of the rail of the chair with the

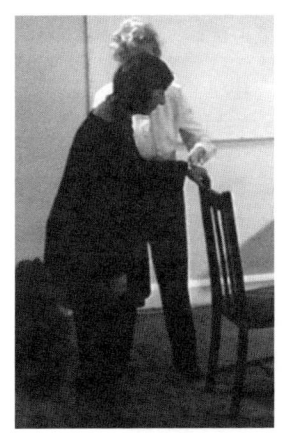

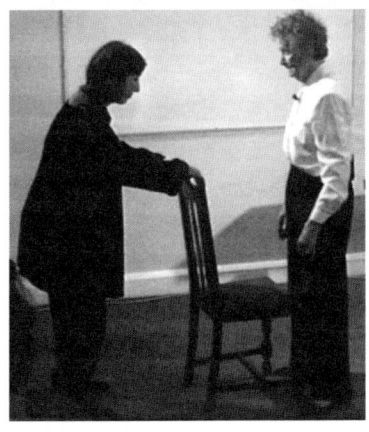

Marjory Barlow teaching hands over back of chair (Regent's College 1998)

second finger opposite the thumb. This allows the armpit to release and the back to widen.

So, when I've got one hand on the rail of the chair I order my wrist in, the pull to the elbow as I think of widening the upper part of the arm as I widen the back. Then I organise the other hand in the same way. After that I come back to my neck, head and back making sure that I'm not stiffening the knees, ankles or toes – I scan myself in other words. Finally, I think of lifting and stretching the piece of wood. And I stay there until I get tired. I wouldn't put a time limit on it – I stay there as long as the whole thing is alive.

Did Alexander ever teach you to try to actively, as it were, stretch the piece of wood?

No, that's a wrong interpretation. The way FM taught it, it was just a direction.

And I note that you like to monitor whether someone is making excess tension by seeing, when the hands are on the chair, whether the arms can still move freely in an up-and-down motion.

FM did this. I generally do it before the thought of lifting and stretching the piece of wood just to make sure that the pupil isn't fixing anywhere.

What variations with hands over the chair did Alexander teach?

Sometimes he would take you on your toes – that was a favourite.

PART 3: THE GROUND RULES

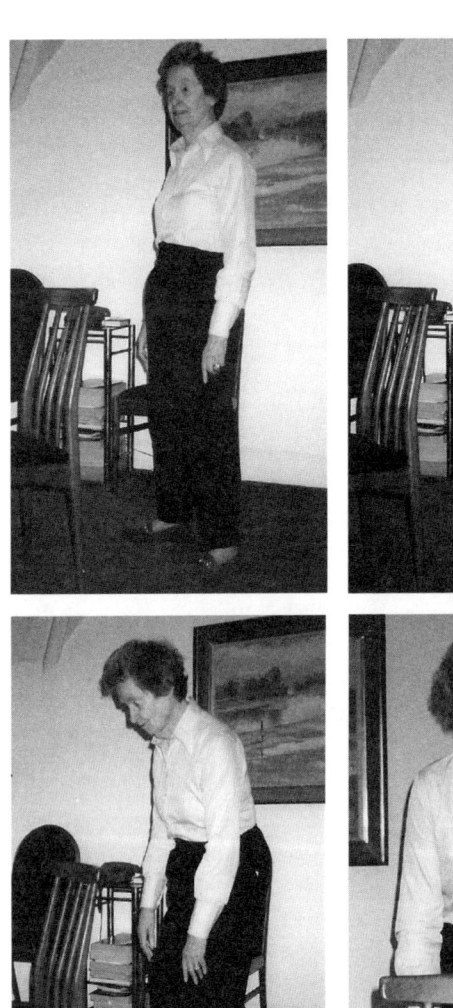

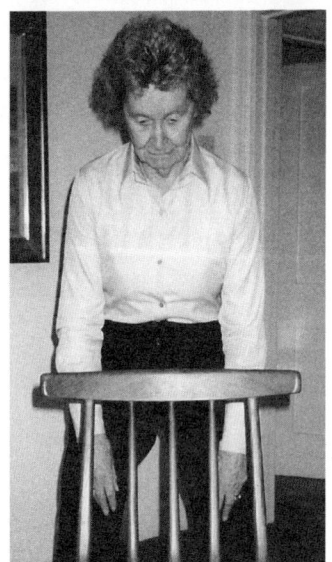

HANDS OVER THE BACK OF A CHAIR

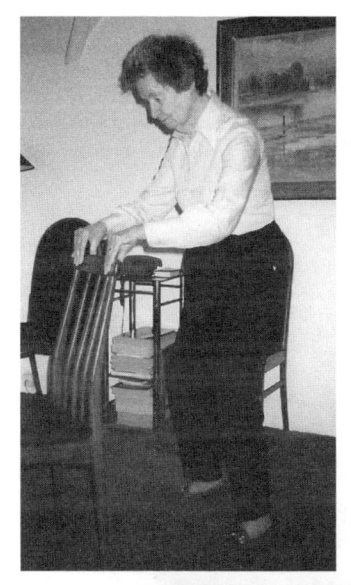

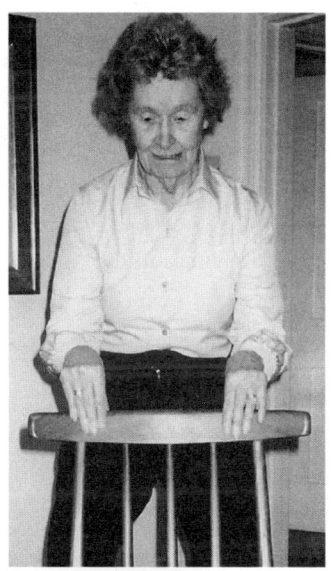

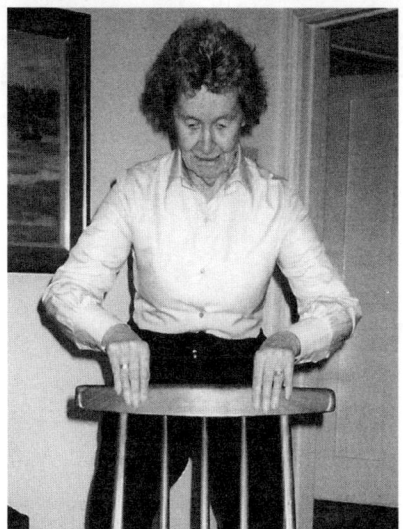

Marjory Barlow demonstrating hands over the back of a chair (1997)

And was hands over the chair something he encouraged the students and pupils to perform on their own?

Oh yes. FM never limited any student to think that you can only do something with a teacher there. The way FM taught was all about showing us how to work on ourselves in different ways.

Perhaps you could explain the relevance of hands over the chair to everyday life.

As I'm sitting here now, I don't think I was aware of my wrists going in or anything like that but I am certainly aware of not gripping in the armpit.

But I find hands over the chair very useful in all manner of activities. When carrying something like a shopping basket, the tendency is to turn the wrist, but if you hold it so that the back of the hand is facing forward it's so much easier. You don't need to completely straighten the arms – you want to have a bit of a bend – and you certainly don't want to lock them. Explaining this to pupils after they have had some experience of hands over the chair often means that they carry things in different ways. I've also found that the orders help many of them in the prevention of shoulder pain.

Using the wall

FM used to tell us that using the wall was particularly useful when working with new pupils, especially when the balance was altering. The wall, in other words, was very reassuring because the pupil couldn't fall. The other purpose of using the wall was to get the lower back back – but not to force it.

So to get organised, you want to stand with your heels about three or four inches from the wall with the feet about hip width apart and turned out as in monkey. You give your orders, and then give yourself a stimulus to go back to the wall – I'm talking about your body not your head. You carry on doing that for a little while, and then allow yourself to go back to the wall. One thing that is interesting to notice is whether one shoulder or buttock hits the wall before the other. Over time any tendency you have along these lines should improve.

All the time you're in contact with the wall, you're giving your orders. Then you give yourself the stimulus to bend the knees. At the same time you are careful to keep your length, and then you bend your knees. This will bring you down the wall a bit while you're trying not to lose stature. In other words, the head should stay where it is – at least in the initial movement. But using the wall is very helpful for the back. Put simply, if you've got a very hollowed back, as you come down the wall your back will come back and become flatter.

You can go down the wall as much as you want to and then decide to give yourself the stimulus to come up again. At this point, you've got to be a bit careful because the tendency is to throw the back in again as you make the return journey. So you notice that tendency and keep it in mind, and then straighten your knees a bit without stiffening and drawing them back. From experience, I've found that the best way to avoid messing the movement up is by telling the knees to go forward from the hips and away from each other as you straighten them.

You can then, if you want, do a little more work by going up on to the toes. And the thing to avoid here – although, of course, this applies to everything we do – is holding the breath as you move. You can stay there for a moment or two before coming down again. And all you do in order to come down is to let the ankles release.

FM never specified anything about the heels directing the movement to the ground – I think other people have brought that idea in but it's not really necessary. It's also very important in the movement to keep monitoring yourself and if, say, you find that you're doing something untoward like pulling your back in, then stop and redirect.

Another variation here is that when you're on your toes you can increase the bending of the knees, which will bring you down the wall a little bit. Of course, you try to maintain your stature as you perform this. When I do it, I don't think of the knees going over the big toes or anything like that, I just think of them going forward from the hips and away from each other.

I find it very useful as the knees straighten once more to give an inhibitory order not to pull the back in. This may or may not work at first. If it doesn't, then just notice it – just be interested in it. After all, the only thing we've got to help us is to do it wrong, and then learn from it. I realise, of course, that this is not the attitude of most people who think that they've

USING THE WALL

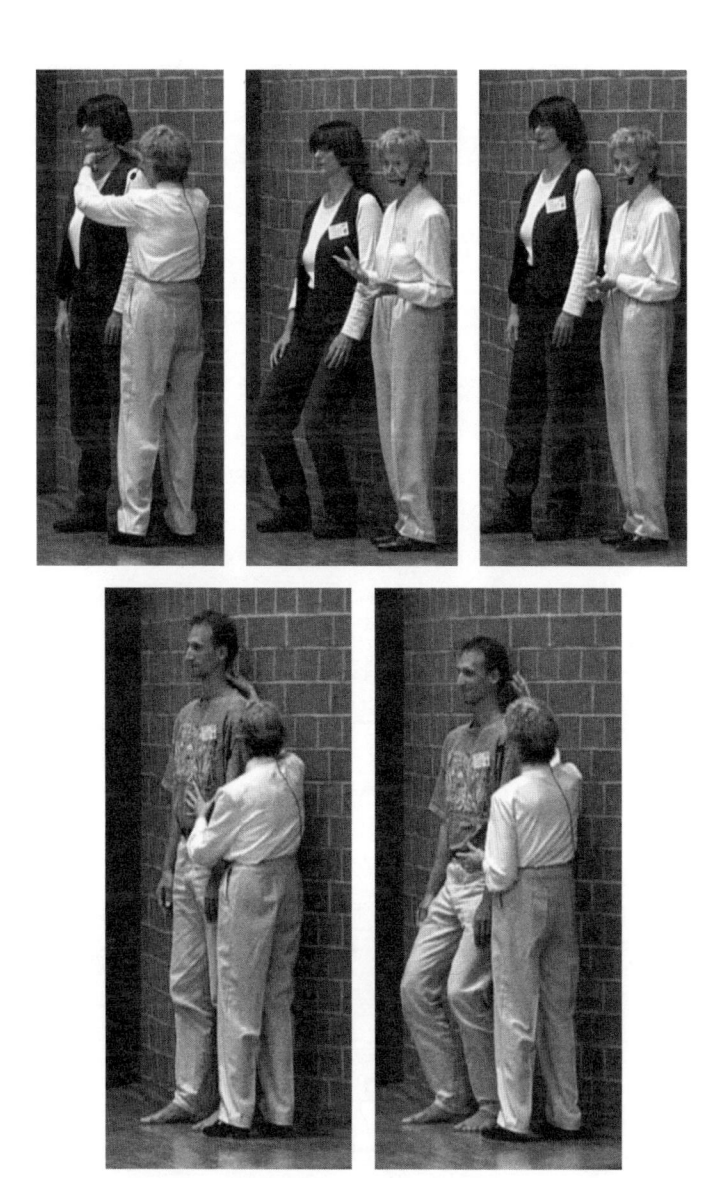

Marjory Barlow demonstrating wall work (Freiburg Congress 1999)

PART 3: THE GROUND RULES

got to be right all the time. Which reminds me of something FM used to say to us: "You are right – there's nothing wrong with any of you. You're all quite perfect, except for what you're doing." That's rather wonderful, isn't it?

FM also used to say that when you've got down the wall – when you bend your knees so that your back is more or less flat – the danger point is when you come up again. He used to tell you that you must try not to pull the back in again. All the time, of course, the head must lead. Pat Macdonald always used to say you've got to think of your head as if it was a football sitting on the top of the spine. Which means you're thinking of the whole head, not just a part of it.

In order to come away from the wall you just let the head lead as if you're going to take a step forward. A lot of people, of course, bend from the hips instead of coming straight forward. So the thing to remember is that all of you comes off the wall with the head just leading.

Will using the wall work if you have the feet parallel as in skiing?

Well, for ordinary life it's always better to have the toes very slightly turned out because it facilitates the movement of the knees. Let's say I've got my feet parallel and I go to put my knees away from each other – I've got to twist my ankle. However, if the feet are slightly turned out, the knees can take the direction over the toes.

Will it affect the efficiency of the movement if you have the feet too far turned out?

Well I suppose it's moderation in all things. It probably wouldn't help if you did a Charlie Chaplin sort of thing.

The wall has also been employed by some teachers to help a pupil perform a monkey. The pupil is to bend the knees and slide down the wall while maintaining length as you've already described. The torso is then inclined forward while the tail remains in contact with the wall. Where did this come from?

Now, this was a practice that was devised by my husband, Bill, rather than FM. It's described in *The Alexander Principle*. Bill was someone who would come up with half a dozen different ideas before lunchtime. It's not something I've ever bothered with very much, but there's certainly nothing wrong with it.

Marjory & Dr Wilfred Barlow (c1975)

The whispered ah

FM taught whispered ah to everyone when he thought they were capable of keeping more than two directions going at once. And he used to emphasise that the beginning of it involved thinking of something funny in order to smile. However, it has to be a genuine smile rather than a grimace. It all has to come from within – you have to smile and then everything releases.

In fact, FM used to say: "If you can't think of something funny to make you smile, you certainly can't give orders." Now, I've never really understood that, but that's certainly what he said. Anyway, once you've got the smile, you place the tip of the tongue to the top of the lower teeth, which flattens the tongue, let the jaw drop and then let the ah come out. FM used to say that the whispered ah sound should come out like gas – in other words, there should be no effort.

Now the jaw is a very interesting joint. And in the whispered ah you're allowing the jaw to fall, but not so that it drops back into the throat. If you put your fingers on the joint just in front of the ears – this is something FM showed us – and let the jaw go forward and open it, a huge great hole appears in the area of the joint. So we were always taught by FM to make sure that the lower jaw is coming forward from the joint to make the necessary space.

People often feel that they need to take a breath for the whispered ah but they don't – there's always loads of air available. It's a problem that asthmatics have: they're actually full of air, but they feel that they can't breathe. It means that they try to get more air into already over-filled lungs. The important thing for an asthmatic is to be brave enough to breathe out. Of course, often this is something which terrifies them but really it's the only way. I've had quite a lot of success with teaching asthmatics – I just explain to them that it's really their feeling that they haven't got any air, even though they've got bags of the stuff. And, as I say, if they can just have the courage to breathe out then they will have a whole new experience, and then they're on their way.

It is important that you make each whispered ah complete and distinct. The main problem people have is that they make too much effort, but the whispered ah should only be as long as you can do it without forcing it. The moment it begins to be an effort, then it's time to stop. But I must stress that it isn't a silent ah – it should be something you can hear. And remember a whisper can be very penetrating.

FM taught whispered ah to people in monkey, standing, sitting, and lying down – whatever was appropriate, really. When you were performing them, he'd have one hand at the front – not on the jaw but on the forehead – and one hand at the back of the head. However, I always teach whispered ah to people when they're lying down so I can see what's happening.

There was no set regime for whispered ah, but FM certainly encouraged us to do them. He used to say, "There's not a single cell in your body which isn't altered when you perform a whispered ah, because the food of the cells is oxygen." And certainly, he did whispered ahs whenever he had a moment. I find I like to do them when I get into bed at night. I lie on my back, give my orders and then do a few. I also do them during the day if I feel a bit tired. But I don't have a rule about how many I will do – I don't say I'm going to do twelve or anything like that – just what's appropriate at the time.

At what point in the breathing cycle does the jaw fall forward? I ask this because I think the assumption that many people make is that the whispered ah should only be performed if plenty of air is available.

Yes, that's a very common belief. From my own experience, I find if I get to the point of doing all of the required things very slowly, and then I find I haven't got any breath I just shut my mouth and start again.

This means that you might find yourself opening the jaw on the inhalation.

That's right, but it doesn't matter. You perform the whispered ah with whatever breath is available. When I was playing Horatio in *Hamlet* I had to learn that even though I felt I didn't have any breath, I actually had a lot in my lungs, which I never normally used. So learning to do great long Shakespearean speeches is one of the most wonderful trainings against that feeling that 'I've got to take a breath.' And, as I say, it's often very surprising how long you can go on for.

So you're not especially concerned whether you're breathing in or out as you prepare for the whispered ah?

No. I'm thinking of my back widening so my lungs can work.

Presumably, this is what Alexander meant when he

talked about the 'satisfactory expansion and contraction of the walls of the thoracic (chest) cavity' in his analysis of the respiratory mechanisms in *Constructive Conscious Control of the Individual* ?

Yes. He wants the pupil to direct the back to widen. That does it for you. You see, everything in this Technique is indirect.

Nevertheless, you do hear Alexander teachers say, "Consciously direct the ribs together" or some such phrase.

FM didn't say anything like that. He might have said, "Release the ribs" but even then it was all about thinking. The beautiful thing about this Technique is that the right thing will be done for you if you get out of the way because that way you're working in accordance with the laws of nature.

Another thing FM would remind you of if you were pinching the nostrils together was to just touch the nose – he would just tap it – to let them widen out.

One interesting variation on the conventional procedure is to allow the jaw to fall open but to keep breathing in and out through the nose, and then at the desired time allow the air to come out through the mouth as a whispered ah.

That's absolutely fine. There's nothing wrong with that as far as I can see.

Did Alexander ever get a pupil to hold the breath – to suspend the breathing if he could detect a significant

degree of misuse while someone was performing the whispered ah?

No. What he would do in those circumstances was to get the pupil to shut the mouth and start all over again, paying particular attention to the neck and head. FM never, ever got us to hold the breath.

Lying down

I don't know exactly when FM started to lie people down but it was certainly being used in Australia before he came to England. He used to say that it's very good to lie down because you don't have to bother about your equilibrium. In fact, I find it particularly useful to introduce it when people start lessons because there is often such a change in the balance. When someone is lying down there is nothing to worry about apart from inhibiting and giving the orders. So it's a very good situation for message giving. But FM wanted people to work on themselves, not just to have a rest. He used to say, "You don't lie down like this to go to sleep – you've got to work."

To get on the floor, FM would get us to squat and then sit. If that was too difficult for people, then he recommended that they should go down on to their knees, and then sit. Then we were instructed to put the knees over and lie on the side before rolling on to the books.

He didn't encourage us to go straight down from a sitting position, as you might with the assistance of a teacher in a lesson, because he thought that was too difficult for most people – they'd stiffen the neck as they went back. And he told us to put the inhibitions in where we wanted to – 'Now, I'm going to roll over' – 'Now, I'm going to move the knees' and so on, as we did each new thing.

Nowadays, people often use a great height of books, but FM told us to use just enough so that the head wasn't falling back, but not so much that the chin was being forced down.

FM said to start with the legs straight out in front of you, but with the knees releasing forward and away. This means, of course, that you then have to get your legs up, which is very difficult to accomplish without twisting or pulling the back up. In order to counteract this, he used to say: "Take plenty of time and give plenty of orders."

The other thing FM used to recommend was that if you found that your back was too arched once your knees were up, just stop, give your orders and bring up one leg at a time and use the arms to embrace or cuddle the legs. Then very gently pull the knees towards you and hold them for a few moments – it uncurls you immediately.

I used to find this a great help with my bad back in the early days when I was having lessons with FM. Of course, you want to be careful how you use your arms and shoulders if you do this – you don't want to cause another problem while trying to sort out the back.

You have devised further ways to move the legs when you are lying down and the legs are out straight in front, in order to minimise the amount of muscular work involved. Can you explain?

Yes. This is something that you can do when you don't have a teacher to help. Basically, you give your orders and with one foot at a time very gently and slowly point the toes forward and then bend the knee towards the ceiling. Once both knees are up you want to allow a little bit of time for the back to settle. If you still think it's necessary to bring the legs up in order to get more release in the lower back then slowly and gently flex the toes upwards, once again moving one leg at a time. Once both legs are in place then you can cuddle them with your arms. When you come to put each leg down you gently flex the toes once again and allow the heel to lead the movement. People are often amazed how much easier it is to move the legs in these ways.

Other than this there were no other adjustments that FM recommended apart from using the hands to adjust the position of the books under the head. But there was to be no lifting of the head or stretching the neck with the hands or anything like that. However, FM used to say that you were to lie on your back, not on the back of your head. If that wasn't happening, you were to give yourself that order to free the neck to allow a better co-ordination to take place.

When you were lying down you were allowed to do what was described in FM's books. So you were to give yourself the stimulus to, say, move an arm. Then, you would say 'no' and pick the arm up from the side and place it, for example, on the tummy. After that, you could put it back again. Alternatively, you could let either one or both knees fall outwards, and then bring one or both back again. So everything was to be done with inhibition and while giving orders.

In general, in lying down the arms were always placed by the side. Always. They were never placed on the tummy except as I've just indicated.

The other thing FM used to get us to do once we'd done quite a bit of work in lying down was to place the fingers against the floating ribs. This acts as a stimulus to encourage widening. And I must emphasise that there is no 'doing' to be done – you're not meant to push the fingers against the ribs or anything like that. There's no need to – the placing of the fingers against the ribs means that it all happens of its own accord. The other thing that FM would get us to do when the hands were placed like that was whispered ah.

If you were a little bit tense, FM would say: "Give yourself a stimulus to turn the head to the right, and then turn it back again. Then turn it to the left, and back again." He recommended that this should be done very slowly and that there should be no lifting the head either with or without the use of the hands. If I do this nowadays, I like to keep the eyes looking out at a particular point on the ceiling and then slowly turn the head from side to side.

So there were little simple movements that could be made that were designed to encourage undoing rather than doing. FM also suggested these little movements because it would stop the mind wandering. In other words, you keep your attention better than if you're just lying there and 'going to sleep' as he put it.

When you were lying down, the directions FM gave us were: 'Neck free, head forward and up, the whole spine to lengthen right up into the head, back to widen, and knees to go up to the ceiling.' The direction for the knees was shorthand for the lengthening from hip joint to the knee, and ankle to the knee.

One of the other things FM used to suggest to us was to say the orders aloud. You were to give these continuously, but not in a gabble. You had to think what the messages were. And giving your orders aloud wasn't just when you were lying down, but when you were working on yourself in other activities as well.

To get up, you turn the head, turn the knees allowing the body to turn to the side, get up onto the knees, sit on your haunches, and then stand up. Simple!

How long did Alexander recommend that you lie down for?

FM didn't lay down rules about how often or for how long lying down should be performed. He left it to your native intelligence and the circumstances of your life. However, I've found from experience that it is best done every day. For most people twenty minutes is an optimum time. Ten minutes, for example, is too short – but you can extend it. It's really a question of how long you can entertain yourself.

What about directions to the arms in lying down? Are they important?

I think so. When I'm lying down, the arms are by the side with wrists in, and I am thinking of a pull to the elbows, widening the upper part of the arms as I widen the back. Sometimes I like to think of space in the armpit as if I have a raw egg there. I then think of the whole hand lengthening from the wrist.

Lying down with arms by the side (2011)

But unlike hands on the back of a chair, you aren't actively straightening the fingers?

No. The sequence I use in lying down is: order the wrists in, the pull to the elbows and the widening of the arms. I get that bigger thing going and then get the thought of my fingers lengthening. I don't start with the fingers. It is an afterthought and very dependent on what the arm is doing.

What about the orders to the knees?

Well, like the arms these are secondary orders. If you want my opinion, I'd say that the legs are slightly more important than the arms, because the legs are all part of the lengthening process whereas the arms are more like appendages.

Locomotion precedes manipulation...

That's absolutely right. That is a very neat way of putting it. I like that.

It's interesting to hear you say that Alexander encouraged the students on the training course to say the orders aloud. Perhaps you could say something more about this.

Basically, you've got to think about what it means when you use words like 'neck to be free' or 'knees to go up to the ceiling'. You have to pay attention to the part you're ordering. It's an intentional mental direction. Of course, how I direct very much depends on what state I'm in.

In that case, it would be useful to know how you would

proceed if you were not in a particularly good state, and also if you were going well.

If I wasn't in a good state, I'd spend quite a lot of time on the neck before adding the head and then the back. But if I'm going fairly well, it's all ongoing. If you're going well, it's a question of picking up when you deviate. You think: 'Hey, what am I doing?' and then proceed accordingly. That's why I've always liked the phrase 'thinking in activity' – it really sums up what the Alexander Technique is all about.

Afterword

When we first met the Technique in the late 1950s the typed list of teachers fitted easily onto a single page, they were all known to each other personally or by repute and had been trained by Alexander or one of his pupils. Since then we have seen a remarkable growth of interest in Alexander's work throughout the world, and an expansion in the number of trained teachers so that we now count them in their thousands. The satisfaction of having been part of this movement of world wide recognition is tempered by concern as to how the Technique is now being taught. It seems to be the case that when any teaching grows in popularity there is a danger that its more subtle aspects tend to be lost.

In an Alexander lesson, because the pupil is led to certain agreeable therapeutic sensory experiences, largely through the teacher's hands, it is difficult not to think that these experiences are the point of the lesson. When we remember Alexander's own circumstances, that to deal with his voice problem he had only his power of observation and his capacity to think, we are reminded that the main purpose of having lessons in the Technique is to develop the ability to work on oneself as a means of correcting habits of misuse, and that it is mainly through thinking that such

AFTERWORD

work is to be undertaken. Alexander's statement, "None of you wants anything mental," sums up a human weakness and is as true today as when he made it.

During our training with Marjory Barlow she often said to us, "If you haven't taught your pupils to work on themselves you have failed as a teacher." This challenge has been almost impossible to live up to and a powerful antidote to complacency. Because of the emphasis she placed on thinking, which in our observation, is the aspect of the Technique most easily lost sight of, the opportunity to hear Marjory's thoughts, skilfully drawn out by Seán Carey's questions, is very timely and should be welcomed by all those with a serious interest in the Alexander Technique.

Adam and Rosemary Nott

Acknowledgments

It is a great pleasure to be able to acknowledge a great deal of support from many quarters. In particular, I would like to thank Dr David Barlow for permission to allow the interviews with his late mother to be printed. I also wish to express my gratitude to him for providing some of the photographs of Marjory, and for taking a photograph of the chair that FM Alexander used for teaching which is in his family's possession.

I would like to thank Angela Barlow for writing the Preface and providing a photograph of Marjory. And I am indebted to Anne Battye for writing the Introduction, which provides fascinating detail on Marjory's training course in the early 1960s. Thanks also to Adam and Rosemary Nott for contributing an Afterword.

I would like to record my gratitude to Ann James for editing the manuscript and Claire Rennie and Kamal Thapen for providing the Index. I am also indebted to author and editor, Dalton Exley, for making many excellent suggestions on content and layout. Additionally, I am very grateful to David Reed for the use of pictures taken from the filmed material of workshops given by Marjory in London in 1989 and Freiburg in 1999 that are included in the book. Thanks are also due to The Society of Teachers of the

Alexander Technique (STAT), which allowed the reproduction of pictures of FM Alexander from the archives.

I would also like to thank Vicki Towers for the design and typesetting of the book.

Finally, the encouragement Kamal Thapen offered in the preparation of the manuscript for publication, for organising the production and printing of the book has been very much appreciated.

Picture Credits

The FM associated pictures on pages 23, 29, 34, 39, 41, 47, 57, 61, 69, 72, 102, 105, 109, 111, 114, 118 and 120 are all the copyright (2011) of The Society of Teachers of the Alexander Technique (STAT) and are from the STAT archives

FM's table picture on page 50, courtesy of the owner, Caroline Dale (MSTAT)

FM's chair picture on page 52, courtesy of Dr David Barlow

George Bernard Shaw and Aldous Huxley pictures on page 54 are the copyright of Corbis Images

Pictures of Marjory Barlow on pages 85, 86, 99, 117 and 129 are reproduced from video clips, courtesy of David Reed (MSTAT)

Marjory Barlow's picture on page 97 and the one of Marjory and Dr Wilfred Barlow on page 131, courtesy of Angela Barlow (MSTAT)

Marjory Barlow pictures on pages 124 and 125, courtesy of Seán Carey (MSTAT)

The lying down picture on page 141, courtesy of Kamal Thapen (MSTAT)

Index

Activity
  Marjory's favourite *89*
  thinking in *143*
Actor *42, 43, 46, 90, 91*
Albert Court *17*
Alexander, AR (Albert Redden) *46, 47, 49*
Alexander, Max *26, 49*
The Alexander Principle (Barlow) *18, 131*
Alexander Teaching Associates (ATA) *11*
America *54, 56, 70, 93*
An Examined Life (Allan-Davies) *12*
Anaemic, George Bernard Shaw *55*
Ankles
  crossed *113*
  going / come back from *101, 103*
  twist your *108*
Antagonistic actions / pulls *76, 88*
Apprenticeship *18, 25*
Arm(s)
  placed by the side *139, 141*
  length of the *121*
  FM unable to straighten his *121*
  using to raise body *115, 116*
Armpit
  clenching in *84*
  gripping in *126*
  imaginary raw egg in *84, 141*
Ashley Place *18, 25, 33, 38, 42, 44, 50-52, 56, 57, 60, 61, 93, 103*
Asthmatic(s) *58, 132, 133*
Attention, quality of *73*
Aunty Mary *45*
Aunty May *45*
Australia *45, 71, 89, 90, 137*

Back pain *19, 56*
Backache *26*
Balance, between hands in teaching *80*
Barlow, Angela *10, 146*
Barlow, Dr David *146*
Barlow, Dr Wilfred (Bill) *9, 10, 15, 17, 18, 94, 131*

Barstow, Marjorie *70*
Bates Method *56*
Battye, Anne *21, 146*
Being, FM's whole *31*
Breath, hold(ing) the *20, 128, 136*
Breathing cycle, in whispered ah *134*
Burton, Don *11*

Calcutta, black hole of *50-52*
Carrington, Dilys *11*
Carrington, Walter *11, 12, 14, 78*
Central School of Speech and Drama *17*
Centre of gravity *77*
Chair
  backwards and forwards *72, 88, 119, 120*
  getting in / out of *32, 66, 78, 88*
  getting out of low *114*
  hands over / on the back of *12, 19, 27, 49, 88, 89, 115, 121-126*
  jump up out of *30*
  rail of *19, 122, 123*
  use in sitting and standing *113, 116, 117, 121*
  vehicle for learning *65*
Chaplin, Charlie *131*
Cherry, taking two bites of the, in monkey *104*
Clinical observation *19*
Conscious control *32, 42*
Constructive Conscious Control of the Individual (Alexander) *25, 135*
Contrary pulls *118*
Corsets *42*
Cross-legged, FM sitting *113, 114*

Davies, Trevor Allan *12*
Derby, Epsom *38*
Dewey, John *41*
Diagnosis *55*
Door handles, in squatting *110*

Elbows, pull to the *75, 141, 142*
End-gaining *18*
Energy, FM's *34, 35, 60*
Eyes
  FM's *33*
  using in teaching *73, 74, 140*

INDEX

Feet
    are at an angle *111*
    drawing the feet back *77, 78*
    level *78*
    turned out vs straight *104, 108, 130*
Floating ribs, fingers on *139*
Floor
    lift off the *103*
    lying on the *54, 110*
    sitting on the *88*
    working on / using the *50, 88, 109*
Food, FM's ideas on *35, 36*
Forward(s)
    and away *95, 128*
    and up *15, 62, 101, 118, 122, 140*
    jaw *132, 134*
    or backwards *72, 88, 89, 94, 115, 119, 120*
    throw the body *90, 98, 100-103*
Freedom to Change (Jones) *82*

Gravity, centre of *77*
Ground rules *12, 15, 18, 19, 28, 97, 98, 100*
Group work, with children *71*

Habit(s)
    bad *32, 72*
    force of *32*
Hamlet *91, 92, 134*
Hand(s)
    back of the *115*
    knuckles of each *115*
    on the back *73, 80, 82*
    over the back of chair *12, 19, 27, 49, 75, 88, 89, 121-126, 142*
    use *17, 72, 74, 80*
    working with *31*
Head(s)
    pull their head(s) back *26, 47, 81*
    to go forward(s) and up *15, 29, 62, 75, 77, 81, 101, 106, 108, 118, 122, 140*
Headache *79*
Heel(s) *127, 128, 139*
Hinge, joints acting as *77*
Hips back *75, 77*
Horse(s) *38, 39, 43, 46, 63*

Huxley, Aldous *41, 53-56*
Huxley, Matthew *53*
Hyde Park, AR thrown off horse *46*

Inhibition *10, 19, 63, 65, 83, 87, 115, 137, 139*
Inner Ear *73*
Interference, with primary control *16, 65, 74*
Irving, Henry *91*

Jaw *132-135*
Joints *15, 28, 62, 77, 79, 106*
Jones, Frank Pierce *83*

Knees
    apart *60, 108*
    apply gentle pressure to *84*
    forward and away *29, 49, 100, 138*
    forward from hips *49, 75, 76, 104, 106, 108, 110, 113, 118, 122, 128*
    to go up to the ceiling *138, 140, 142*
Knuckles *115*

Lang, Matheson *90*
Leg(s)
    are out straight *138*
    crossed *108, 113, 114*
    cuddle the *138, 139*
    take a *74, 83, 87*
Lesson(s)
    course of *54, 58, 62, 66, 71*
    first *17, 24, 78, 79*
    frequency *55, 59*
    individual *11, 71*
    introductory *58, 71*
    sufficient *76*
Lifting and stretching, rail of chair *123*
Little School *25, 27, 51, 71*
Lunge *105, 111, 112*
Lungs *133, 134*
Lying down *12, 13, 27, 83-85, 87, 133, 137-142*

Macdonald, Patrick (Pat) *11, 14, 28, 70, 71, 91, 111, 130*
Macdonald, Peter *70*

149

INDEX

Man's Supreme Inheritance
(Alexander) *37, 49, 76, 78, 119*
Meaning, lack of in life *37*
Means whereby *14, 16-20*
Mechanical advantage *109*
Meningitis *39*
Merchant of Venice, The 90-92
Migraines *24, 26*
Mind wandering *140*
Mirrors, FM's use of *36, 65*
Misuse / misusing *18-20, 37, 59, 63, 136*
Monkey *12, 16, 19, 20, 27, 49, 72, 76, 80, 88, 96, 100, 104-108, 113, 121, 127, 131, 133*
Movement, importance of *119*

Neck
  head back *16, 75, 79, 80, 82, 87, 95, 112, 123*
  release *15, 81*
  to relax *77*
  stiffening *20, 77, 81, 119, 137*
  stretching *139*
New Zealand *89*
Nicholls, John *12*
Nostrils, pinching the *135*
Nott, Adam *11, 145, 146*
Nott, Rosemary *145, 146*
Numbers, painting by *75*

Old Vic *90*
Operational verification *30*
Orders
  aloud *140, 142*
  FM saying *29*
  guiding *74*
  singing our *10*
  verbalise *30*
Orthopaedic (surgery) *89*

Pain *19, 25, 26, 56, 126*
Penhill *39, 71, 72, 114*
Piano, Marjory's love of *36*
Pierce Jones, Frank *82*
Polio (Lulie Westfeldt) *91*
Position
  correct standing *76, 78*

  erect/upright *77, 120*
  fixed *62*
  of mechnical advantage *109*
  static *96*
Posture, FM critical of term *62*
Pressing, down into the floor *63*
Pressure
  apply *82, 83*
  time *64*
  to the knees *84*
Prevention of shoulder pain *126*
Primary Control *16, 75*
Primrose Hill *11*
Procedures, Alexander *19, 20, 28, 121*
Process
  inhibitory *87*
  learning *27, 30, 63*
  mysterious *84*
Pulls, contrary *118*
Pulling down *10, 87, 94, 102, 114, 119*
Pulse, FM's *43*
Push
  the back out of the chair *119*
  the fingers against the ribs *139*

Reaction(s)
  emotional *65*
  first *32, 33*
Re-educational *51, 63*
Relationship
  head-neck-back *75, 82*
  reciprocal *75*
Relax, neck *77*
Religion, FM's attitude to *39, 40*
Respiratory mechanisms *135*
Ribs
  direct the *135*
  fingers against the *139, 140*
  floating *139*
  release the *135*

Sadler's Wells *90*
School, Little *25, 27, 51, 71*
Scoliosis, singer with *58*
Self-worth, FM's sense of *40, 41*
Sensory appreciation *14, 30, 48*
Shakespearean speeches *134*
Shaw, George Bernard (GB) *41, 52-55*

INDEX

Shoulder(s)
    back and down *82*
    prevention of pain *126*
    take a *74, 83, 84*
Simple but not easy, the Alexander Technique *33*
Sitting on the floor giving a lesson *88, 109*
Skiing, feet parallel *130*
Slump(ed) *115*
Smile, in whispered ah *132*
Spine
    football sitting on top of the *130*
    s-shaped *25*
Squatting *108-110*
Stamina *26, 35*
Stammer *61, 62*
Static position *95*
Stature *100, 104, 111, 127, 128*
Stiffening
    knees *103, 123, 128*
    neck *20, 77, 81*
Sub-occipital muscles *81*

Table, FM's teaching *50*
Table Cape, Tasmania *45*
Tasker, Irene *25, 27, 103*
Tasmania *35, 45*
Teaching
    couch *18*
    introductory classes *71*
    AR and FM methods *48, 49*
    FM's room *51*
Temper, FM's *34*
Thinking in activity *143*
Throat, whispered ah *132*
Throwing the body forward *103*
Thumb
    in armpit *84*
    second finger opposite *123*
    too much, in using hands in teaching *80*
Toes
    flex the *138, 139*
    going up on to *27, 49, 88-90, 98-100, 103, 123, 128*
    lifting off floor *103*
    knees over (big) toes *128, 130*
    turned out *104, 130*
Tongue
    flatten the *132*
    tip of the *132*
Torso, angle of *121, 131*
Tree, Viola *91*

Universe, meaning in the *40*
Upright, sitting (position) *49, 77, 120*
Using small movements *120*

Vampires *66*
Victorian stool *50*
Vocal performance *58*
Voice, FM recovered his *47*

Wales, holidays in *43*
Walker, Dick *15*
Walker, Elisabeth *15*
Walking
    backwards whilst taking hands *110*
    FM *102*
    pressing down on the floor *63*
    teaching *103*
Wall
    using the *88, 94, 127-131*
    work *129, 130*
Webb, Ethel *30, 51, 59*
Westfeldt, Lulie *47, 91*
Westminster Cathedral *51*
Whispered ah *12, 13, 16, 19, 49, 88, 106, 132-136, 140*
Whittaker, Erika *43*
Wine, FM and *38, 44*
Wodeman, Joyce *15*
Work
    lying down *27, 83, 85, 87, 139*
    on self *17, 64, 94, 137, 144*
    preparatory *80, 82*
Working, new ways of *88*
Wrist(s)
    in *75, 88, 123, 126, 141, 142*
    lengthening from the *141*
    tendency to turn *126*

Zen
    master *84*
    type *38*

Biographical notes

Marjory Barlow (1915 – 2006) was the niece of FM Alexander, the originator of the Alexander Technique. She began a course of lessons with her uncle in 1932, and then in 1933 was invited to join the first training course, which had opened in 1931. Marjory also had lessons and worked with FM Alexander's brother, Albert Redden Alexander. Along with her husband, Dr Wilfred Barlow, she opened an Alexander Technique teacher training course in 1950. After she retired from training in 1979 she continued giving lessons and small classes for teachers and students at her flat in Primrose Hill. She also gave masterclasses for Alexander teachers at a number of Alexander Technique international conferences. Marjory was chair of the Society of Teachers of the Alexander Technique (STAT) from 1964 to 1966 and from 1996 to 1998.

Seán Carey gained a PhD in social anthropology at the University of Newcastle-upon-Tyne. He then trained at Alexander Teaching Associates in London from 1983 to 1986. He currently teaches in London and Hertfordshire. He is co-author of *Explaining the Alexander Technique* and *Personally Speaking* (both with Walter Carrington) and *The Alexander Technique* (with John Nicholls). He is a member of the Society of Teachers of the Alexander Technique.